The StayRetired™ Model

Bonnie

Great to have you as a client. Looking to help you retire and Stay Retired.

Joe E Ray
5/5/2024

704 935-2554

THE STAYRETIRED™ MODEL
How to Retire, Stay Retired™, and Never Be Forced to Go Back to Work
Copyright © 2024 Joe Roseman, Jr.
All rights reserved.
ISBN: 978-1-956220-78-0

www.ExpertPress.net

The information provided in this book is for informational purposes only and is not intended to be a source of advice or credit analysis with respect to the material presented. The information and/or documents contained in this book do not constitute legal or financial advice and should never be used without first consulting with an insurance and/or a financial professional to determine what may be best for your individual needs.

The publisher and the author do not make any guarantee or other promise as to any results that may be obtained from using the content of this book. You should never make any investment decision without first consulting with your own financial advisor and conducting your own research and due diligence. To the maximum extent permitted by law, the publisher and the author disclaim any and all liability in the event any information, commentary, analysis, opinions, advice, and/or recommendations contained in this book prove to be inaccurate, incomplete, or unreliable or result in any investment or other losses.

Although the author and publisher have made every effort to ensure that the information in this book was correct at press time, the author and publisher do not assume and hereby disclaim any liability to any party for any loss, damage, or disruption caused by errors or omissions, whether such errors or omissions result from negligence, accident, or any other cause.

Content contained or made available through this book is not intended to and does not constitute legal advice or investment advice, and no attorney-client relationship is formed. The publisher and the author are providing this book and its contents on an "as is" basis. Your use of the information in this book is at your own risk.

Editing by Emmett O'Neill
Copyediting by Lori Price
Proofreading by Heather Dubnick
Text design and composition by Emily Fritz
Cover design by Casey Fritz

The StayRetired™ Model

How to Retire, StayRetired™, and Never Be Forced to Go Back to Work

Joe Roseman Jr.

Joe Roseman, Jr.
CRPC, CDP, NSSA, ChFEBC
Founder/Investment Advisor

StayRetired™ Wealth Strategies
5960 Fairview Road, Suite 400
Charlotte, NC 28210

(704) 935-2553
jroseman@stayretiredwealth.com
www.stayretiredwealth.com

Dedication

Authoring a book is an arduous task. There have been numerous folks who have been instrumental in helping me reach a point in my career where I was confident that putting all of this information in writing could have a real impact on those who read this manuscript.

So let me thank some of those folks: my former business partners, Todd Curry at 2nd Half Strategies and Jeremy Shipp and the late Kyle Winkfield, at OWRS and Retirement Capital Planners. These three gentlemen inspired, educated, and trained me in the financial services business. There are others, but these three had the most impact.

Thanks to Emmett O'Neill, who translated my thoughts into this book and the editors at Paperback Expert who brought my thoughts to life.

Personally, my mother, Jean Roseman and my late father, Joe Roseman, Sr., have been lifelong Godly examples and inspirations. My dad allowed me to dream and I think about his impact on my life and my character daily. My mom encouraged me to get a job, which inspired me to open my own business when the job I was looking for just never appeared. "Maw" has been the rock of our family since Dad passed away in 1994. They both inspired me to build a business and life based on solid principles of caring and financial education.

I thank my assistant, Vicky Chastain, who started out as a part-time secretary and has become an integral part of our company over the last fourteen years.

And to my wife, Debbie Jean McCall Roseman, who I met at Myrtle Beach in 1982 at the old Studebaker's, where she asked me to dance. We married in March of 1988. She is the mother of two wonderful children, Melissa and Rhett. Also, importantly, she helped me to become the man that I am and to build the business that we have today. I love you, Debbie Jean.

Finally, to all of the clients that we have developed and met though Lincoln Financial, Roseman Financial, OWRS, Retirement Capital Planners and the clients we will continue to service and meet though StayRetired Wealth Strategies. Thank you for having the confidence and trust in us to help you fulfill your retirement dreams.

Contents

Introduction		1
1	It's Not a Budget, It's a Spending Plan	13
2	Income Planning Part 1	25
3	Income Planning Part 2	45
4	Asset Protection and Investment Planning	61
5	How to Structure Your Assets to Minimize Income Taxes	77
6	How to Plan and Save for Post-Retirement Fun	93
7	Reviewing Long-Term Healthcare Choices	103
8	Medicaid Planning	121
9	While You're Alive and After You're Gone	135
10	Legacy and Life Insurance Planning	149
Conclusion		161
About the Author		171

Introduction

*"Always plan ahead.
It wasn't raining when Noah built the ark."*
– Richard Cushing

I've never been more certain of my calling in financial planning, but you may be surprised to hear this wasn't always the case. While my success has been built on helping others plan for a prosperous future, the truth is I, like most folks, once had no idea what I was going to do.

Back in 1981, after graduating from the University of North Carolina at Chapel Hill, I found myself at a crossroads. Despite attending over fifty on-campus interviews, all I had to show for my effort was a stack of rejection letters. I've never been one to take things lying down, so instead of feeling sorry for myself, I got up and kept moving. Well, when God closes a window, he opens a door, and I ended up stumbling upon the insurance business. Though I'll admit, at the time, it was less out of passion and more out of necessity.

I worked for Art Williams at A.L. Williams and Associates, a business now known as Primerica Financial Services. The company's philosophy during that time could best be summed up by the phrase, "Buy term and invest the difference." While it may sound simple, I appreciated their straightforward approach. Let me tell you, it got results. I started getting deeper into the financial world, inspired largely by Art Williams himself. (I recommend his speech titled "Just Do It" for a taste of this inspiration.) After a brief time, I decided this might be the path for me. I got my securities license and made my first official steps into the world of finance. However, my newfound passion waned, and I began to feel directionless and uncertain about my path.

So, I moved on. I got married to the love of my life, Debbie, and dabbled in various roles to make ends meet. From the mortgage business to selling swimming pools, I tried my hand at a number of different industries. In 1986, I ventured into the car business, where I remained until 1993. I wore many hats during that time, working primarily as a salesman and a lease and finance manager. But don't let the car salesman title worry you; I have been entirely healed from that terrible experience! Deciding this industry wasn't quite right for me either, I continued my search.

The next twist in my career had the most profound impact on my future. I entered the cemetery business in Charlotte, North Carolina. Our job was to assist families in planning their final resting place, helping them choose the burial space, vault, marker, and everything else they would need to honor their departed loved ones. This experience was rewarding because I felt I was removing a significant burden from grieving families, ensuring they didn't need to make difficult decisions in the midst of their sorrow.

Then, in 1999, a pivotal experience made me reconsider my path. I had been working with a lovely couple, Calvin and Maria. After I assisted them in preplanning their funeral arrangements, Calvin sadly passed away. Every time Maria visited Calvin's grave, she'd pop by our office. We'd chat, share stories, and, in time, became friends. When I received the call about Maria's passing, I knew I had to help her children, Steve, Sam, and Sally, with the final procedures.

I still remember that rainy Tuesday as the siblings gathered in my office. The mood was bleak, and there was no denying the tension in the air. Despite Maria's thoughtful planning, one piece remained unpaid: the opening and closing of the grave, which amounted to $550. The atmosphere grew even more strained when the bill was presented. Sam glanced at his newly acquired cell phone, Steve stared blankly, and Sally broke down in tears.

That moment was a wake-up call for me. I knew, then and there, I wanted to provide more than just end-of-life financial arrangements. Watching this family struggle with a $550 bill during such a tough time, I realized how good financial guidance could have prevented this. I wanted families to be prepared, to never be caught off guard by unforeseen expenses. I yearned to build relationships with entire families and make sure they always had a financial plan in place. I wanted to make a difference, to ensure that no family ever found themselves in the same situation as Steve, Sam, and Sally. This realization was the driving force that propelled me back into financial services in 2000.

The Dot-Com Bubble and My First Clients

The financial world I was entering at this time can best be described as euphoric but unstable. The late 1990s saw the stock market riding a wave of optimism. The potential of the internet and burgeoning technology companies led to an unprecedented boom, and tech stocks seemed to be on an unstoppable journey upward. On March 10, 2000, the NASDAQ composite index peaked at an astounding 5048.62. Little did we know, this was a peak not reached again until April 23, 2015—more than fifteen years later.

From 2000 to 2002, the market dropped dramatically, with the NASDAQ losing more than 78 percent of its value. This financial trauma was compounded in 2001 with a heart-wrenching event that shook not only the US, but the entire world. The September 11 attacks shuttered the New York Stock Exchange and sent waves of uncertainty throughout America. When trading resumed four days later, the market had plunged by 643.03 points, a staggering drop of 7.13 percent in a single day. All told, trillions of dollars in market value were lost in just a few days. Over the next few years, numerous companies went bankrupt, and average citizens were left wondering whether their retirement funds would ever recover.

During this turbulent time, I met my longest-standing clients, John and Becky. In October of 2002, the very month the market hit its postcrash bottom, John and Becky approached me for life insurance. They were about to be married and living in Charlotte, North Carolina, where they had just purchased a house. Like many people, they had recently experienced substantial market losses. Consequently, our discussions quickly pivoted from life insurance to the broader theme of wealth protection.

John told me right off the bat, "We don't want to lose another dime if we can help it." Wasting no time, I got to work transitioning the IRAs they had accumulated from prior employment into a fixed index annuity. This ensured their funds remained safe from loss, growing as the stock market climbed. Needless to say, they were happy, and I'm proud to say they've been with us ever since.

Years have passed since our first meeting, and we've led John and Becky through a myriad of life events and challenges. From a property purchase in Myrtle Beach and the loss of Becky's job to full-time relocation and John's impending retirement, we've served as their steadfast financial navigators.

I can recall a profound conversation I had with John during one of our regular annual reviews. He began by expressing his mounting frustrations with his job, complaining about his boss and the frequent management changes. As I do with all my clients, I patiently listened, then posed a simple question: "Why not just quit?" My clients are smart, and I don't like to beat around the bush. John was quiet for a long moment, and I could tell he was afraid to answer. Finally, he said how he was truly feeling: "I'm scared." His response revealed a vulnerability many folks feel when it comes to work and financial security. Luckily for him, the right financial planner helped to lay this fear to rest. I knew their situation inside and out and told him exactly how to proceed. Having evaluated their finances, I let him know, with my help, he was already well-positioned for retirement.

Of course, I've realized financial readiness is just one side of the coin; you must also be emotionally ready for retirement. This led me to the advice I now give to all my clients: "For this to work, I need you to trust me. If you're contemplating significant financial decisions, it's essential that you loop me in." Now I'm not saying to call me up before dropping some money on a nice dinner—I'm talking about the big choices in life, like purchases, refinancing, investments. If large sums are being moved, I want to be there to make sure the plane lands safely.

When clients don't keep me clued into their moves, their results may not be ideal. In John's case, his fear may have been rooted more in his own missteps, especially those he left me out of. One of the most significant examples was a land-flipping venture in 2007, which, during the 2008 housing collapse, resulted in a loss of $150,000. Had he consulted me, he may have avoided this mistake, thereby feeling more financially comfortable and less trapped in his job.

Despite these missteps, I still cherish our yearly visits to the beach with John and Becky, even twenty-one years later. Their story exemplifies our mission: to help clients retire and stay retired. To make sure this happens, I designed the StayRetired™ planning model. I've written this book to guide you through the ten StayRetired™ steps and show you just how effective this model is. Each chapter will break down these steps into their core concepts and show you precisely how they work.

StayRetired™ Planning Model

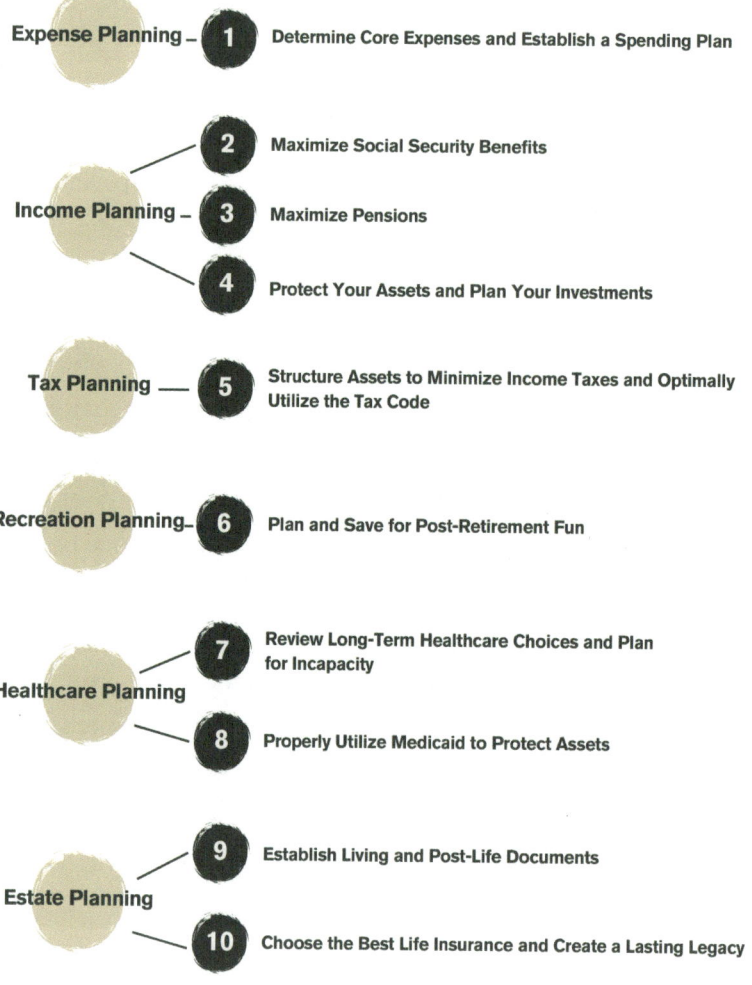

- **Expense Planning** — 1. Determine Core Expenses and Establish a Spending Plan
- **Income Planning**
  - 2. Maximize Social Security Benefits
  - 3. Maximize Pensions
  - 4. Protect Your Assets and Plan Your Investments
- **Tax Planning** — 5. Structure Assets to Minimize Income Taxes and Optimally Utilize the Tax Code
- **Recreation Planning** — 6. Plan and Save for Post-Retirement Fun
- **Healthcare Planning**
  - 7. Review Long-Term Healthcare Choices and Plan for Incapacity
  - 8. Properly Utilize Medicaid to Protect Assets
- **Estate Planning**
  - 9. Establish Living and Post-Life Documents
  - 10. Choose the Best Life Insurance and Create a Lasting Legacy

In over thirty years of experience as a dedicated financial advisor, I have continued to learn and develop my set of professional tools. Over the years, I've pursued numerous credentials to hone my expertise and serve my clients better. These credentials include:

- **Chartered Retirement Planning Counselor (CRPC):** This credential focuses on comprehensive financial planning, not just narrow specialties. Many claim the title "financial planner," but in reality, they are primarily insurance sellers or investment advisors. The CRPC course equipped me to thoroughly understand a client's expenses, income, investments, and estate plan, thus crafting a tailored strategy unique to their financial landscape.
- **National Social Security Advisor (NSSA):** Coupled with fifteen years of experience teaching Social Security maximization strategies through seminars and webinars, this designation enhances my ability to help clients extract maximum benefits from Social Security.
- **Chartered Federal Employee Benefits Consultant (ChFEBC):** With substantial experience aiding federal employees in their financial planning, the ChFEBC credential provides me with a deep understanding of the

federal benefits program, ensuring I can offer these clients specialized and informed advice.

- **Certified Dementia Practitioner (CDP):** As my clientele has aged and as I've engaged with their families, understanding dementia from both a practical and financial perspective has become crucial.[1]

In addition to these qualifications, I've helped educate the public through multiple avenues, including over fifty appearances on our local CBS affiliate WBTV's *Weekend Morning News Show*. I've also contributed to prominent media outlets such as *Time Magazine, US News and World Report,* TheStreet, Investopedia, Credit.com, and Wisebread. These articles can be found on my website: StayRetiredWealth.com.

So why does this all matter to you, the reader? Because in the upcoming chapters, you're not *just* going to learn about numbers or market trends. I'm going to show you the art of intuitive retirement planning, breaking down how to personalize your financial plan and address your unique needs. It's my goal to illustrate just how beneficial informed decision-making can be and share a few stories of client successes and some cautionary tales! (Client names have been changed to protect their privacy, but their stories are true.) From breaking down

---

[1] Designations indicated do not constitute an endorsement or approval of any government agency.

Social Security strategies to navigating the challenges of aging, each chapter is designed to empower you to craft your own unique financial narrative. By the end, you'll have a complete understanding of how to retire and, more importantly, how to StayRetired™.

Let's get started!

1
It's Not a Budget, It's a Spending Plan

How to Determine Your Core Expenses

At the start of my workshops, I often ask the audience, "What's the first question your financial planner is going to ask you?" The answers I get usually revolve around how much money they have in the bank or how much they have invested. While these are important questions, the answers won't help us form the foundation of a good retirement plan. Actually, the first question I ask my clients is, "What are your expenses?" While it isn't sexy, understanding your expenses is essential if you want to have a successful spending plan in retirement. It's like building a house: sure, everyone is excited about the design or the furniture they'll get to put inside, but without a solid foundation, the whole structure is going to fall down. The same holds true for financial planning: *Without* knowing your expenses and creating a solid spending plan, staying retired is going to be a massive challenge.

You may be asking yourself, "Spending plan? Do you mean budget?" Well, no. I prefer the term "spending plan" over "budget" because—let's be honest here—who wants to live on a budget? You've worked hard for your money, and you deserve to spend it. A spending plan can ensure that you allocate your resources properly, allowing you to live life to the fullest. But one issue I frequently run into with my clients is a disconnect between what they believe they spend and what they actually spend. I'll give you an example.

Last July, brand-new clients visited our office for their first appointment; let's call them Sam and Ginny. We sat down to figure out their expenses. Sam told me, "I spend about $5,000 a month and I bring in $7,000, but it seems like I'm barely able to save anything." I asked Sam, "If you're making $7,000 and spending $5,000, but none of it's being saved, where is the $2,000 going? That money isn't just disappearing into thin air." This is where we get to play detective a bit. Let's talk about how you can accurately identify your expenses and a few ways most folks end up missing the mark.

Identifying Your Major Expenses

Let's first look at the most significant spending categories. For most people, these categories include:

- **Housing:** We all need somewhere to live, and housing can make up a sizable portion of your expenses. If you own your house, you'll need to determine how much your monthly and yearly mortgage payment is. This will be decided by a combination of your principal, interest, property taxes, and homeowner's insurance. If you rent, you'll calculate your yearly costs based on how much you pay each month, in addition to extra charges some renters pay, such as parking, garbage disposal, etc.
- **Utilities:** Whether you rent or own, you'll likely have to pay utilities each month (though some renters have utilities included). Utilities can include a wide variety of costs such as electricity, water, gas, waste disposal, heating and cooling, internet, cable, and landlines. These expenses may be variable based on your usage level or location.
- **Medical:** Medical costs will vary depending on your specific needs (a topic we cover more extensively in a later chapter) and what type of medical insurance you are utilizing, as well as how their deductibles are structured. When you

have access to Medicare, you may need to pay for Medicare Part B, Medicare supplements, and any out-of-pocket costs. These out-of-pocket costs will differ from person to person, but in general, you'll want to look at what you're spending each month on doctor visits, medications, and at-home care.

- **Insurance:** In addition to your medical insurance, you'll want to consider other insurance plans as well. This means accounting for homeowner's insurance, renter's insurance, life insurance, auto insurance, and any other type you utilize. Some of these costs may fall into other categories, so you'll decide how to divide it up in your specific spending plan. Be careful not to count certain items twice. For instance, if you calculate your homeowner's insurance as part of your housing costs, don't count it again as an insurance cost.
- **Food:** Everyone's got to eat, and you'd be surprised how much of your income is consumed by food costs. You'll want to tally up how much you spend on groceries each month, how often you go out to restaurants, and how much you spend on getting food delivered. Make sure to include everything: beverages, snack foods, even the occasional dessert. Believe me, it all adds up.
- **Transportation:** The last major category to consider is transportation costs. Your expenses will vary depending on where you live, what you drive,

and whether you own your vehicle outright. If you have a personal vehicle, costs to consider include fuel, auto insurance, repairs, maintenance, fees (like getting your vehicle registered), taxes, and, if you don't own your car, auto payments. If you take public transportation or rideshare services or if you utilize a medical transportation service, you'll need to calculate what you expect to pay on a monthly basis.

These likely don't account for the entirety of your costs, but it's a good place to start when establishing your spending plan. Getting the exact numbers will involve looking at your bank and credit card statements. Personally, I recommend using a credit card for every expense possible, as long as you pay off your cards each month. Almost all of the expenses above can be put on a credit card and help build up a solid credit score. A credit card also provides an additional layer of fraud protection. Another perk can be rewards such as airline miles, cashback, and travel points.

Important: *If you use this strategy, be sure to pay off your card balance each month to avoid nasty interest charges.*

Hidden Costs We Often Overlook

The question now is: What are we forgetting? If you tally up all your expenses and are still left wondering where your money goes, it means we need to dive a bit deeper. While it's easy to remember the payments you are making on a regular basis, some expenditures can slip through the cracks. One of the most common reasons for this "expense amnesia" is the frequency with which we pay specific bills. Think of the payments made on a one-time, seasonal, quarterly, and annual basis. Many of these are set up on an auto-pay system, making it very understandable for them to slip our minds. Here are some examples of these expenses:

One-Time Expenditures
- Large purchases like new furniture, a vehicle, or major appliances
- Out-of-pocket medical expenses, such as elective procedures or dental work
- Upgrades to your home, such as a new air conditioning system or kitchen
- Home repairs or modifications, ranging from fixing up your garage door or roof to the addition of ramps and grab bars, making your home safer and more accessible

Seasonal Expenditures
- Gifts for loved ones, especially the grandchildren, for Christmas, other holidays, or special occasions (such as birthdays)
- Travel expenses, including airfare, vacation lodging and meals, and anything else trip-related

- Seasonal maintenance for your property, which will vary depending on where you live and the season but may include snow and leaf removal, tree trimming, lawn services, etc.

Quarterly Expenses
- Quarterly Medicare premiums (if you are not yet on Social Security) and any quarterly out-of-pocket medical costs
- For those with investment income or who are self-employed, you may make quarterly tax payments to avoid penalties with the IRS

Annual Expenses
- Life and homeowner's insurance premiums
- Property tax payments (when not already part of your mortgage)
- Yearly fees to clubs, services, subscriptions, or software

Separating Wants from Needs: What's Essential and What's Extra?

This is where the spending plan gets really personal. While there are certain elements of your spending plan that are nonnegotiable (housing, food, transportation, etc.), other pieces may not be as essential. This doesn't mean fun and leisure aren't important; in fact, far from it. Not only that, but what you consider a necessity will likely differ from what others consider necessities. It's up to you to determine what is a vital part of your lifestyle and what you can do without. For example, some people are fine pulling the plug on cable and having a few subscription services. For me, I'm currently in the process of building a house two thousand feet off the closest main road, and I'm still dead set on getting cable out there. I put ESPN in my "essentials" category, and I'm not going to mess around with a bunch of different satellite or subscription packages. While some may consider cable a luxury, I consider it a necessity—it's why I account for it in my spending plan.

Deciding what is essential is all about the lifestyle you've grown accustomed to and what improves your quality of life. What type of car you drive is a common example. Personally, I don't care for luxury cars. As long as it's dependable and gets me where I need to go, that's all that matters to me. This perspective allows me to save money in the transportation department, which I can allocate to other categories. Now for you, a car may be everything, which is perfectly fine. Don't let anyone tell you that you don't need to drive a new BMW; if it makes you happy, then it is absolutely a necessity. The same goes for membership at the local country club, the occasional meal at a five-star-rated restaurant, or a vintage bottle of wine for a special occasion. The bottom line is if you can make space in your spending plan, then, by all means, make the purchase.

The issue comes when you *can't* fit it into your spending plan. Now, I'm never going to tell you how to live your life. In fact, I go out of my way to avoid telling my clients how to spend their money, just like I don't want anyone to tell me how to spend mine. My clients are smart, and they got to where they are in life by making intelligent financial decisions. What I will do is point out ways to achieve your goal, which for most of my clients is to retire and StayRetired™. If you tell me you are generating $6,000 a month in income and spending $7,000, then you mention how you visit a steakhouse every night, my advice is going to be pretty clear-cut. That's not to say you have to stop going to the steakhouse, but if it's essential to you, we're going to have to find ways to save money in other areas.

One of the Easiest Areas to Cut: Vice Spending

If you are looking to eliminate expenses, one of the best places to start is vice spending. Again, I'm not saying you have to avoid the top shelf here. I'm not judging anyone who likes to have a good bottle of whiskey now and again. But if you are spending a big chunk of your money on liquor or cigarettes, you have to ask yourself, *is this essential?* Not only are you eating into your income, but you're likely compounding your healthcare costs. Vice spending tends to significantly decrease your available funds. In most cases, this money could be better spent creating memorable nights with loved ones (instead of nights you can't remember).

Let me give you an example of a client who encountered this exact problem. He retired and told us he needed an income of $4,000 a month. We looked at his lifestyle, housing situation, and all of his other costs. After his expenses were tallied, it seemed like he would have no problem staying retired, so we set up everything he needed. Two months later, I woke up on a Saturday morning to a flashing light on my voicemail. This client had called me up late the night before while sitting by the pool with a cocktail and was absolutely lighting me up. Clearly drunk and cussing up a storm, he screamed into the phone (among other things) how I had "messed him up good." He claimed he didn't have enough money to live off and put the blame squarely on my shoulders.

I don't take kindly to someone cursing at me or accusing me of something I didn't do. But I'm a professional, so I called him back and calmly told him to come in the next week with his checking account statements. When we sat down for our meeting, I calculated what he was actually spending, and it was quite a bit more than he had previously claimed. Turns out, he was spending a whopping *$1,000 a month* on liquor. Let me repeat the number: that's $1,000 a month, just on liquor. Not only that, but his income was also higher than he said (due to some changes he had made in his pension, which he did not disclose to me). I can't be entirely sure why he lied to me, but if I had to guess, I would say it was to hide the extra vice spending costs.

Now, I may have been able to forgive the drunken rant or the excess boozing bill this client was racking up, but I absolutely will not work with clients who lie to me. At the end of our annual agreement, I had to terminate our relationship. If someone isn't honest with me, then there is just no way I can help them establish a viable financial plan. This is another way vice spending can really drag you down: If you can't be honest with yourself (or your financial planner) about where your money is going, you will likely have an emotional and exhausting struggle to StayRetired™.

The Other Side of Spending: Income Planning

We've talked about where your money is going, so let's discuss where it is coming from. I always ask my clients, "Why do you work?" In the thirty-plus years I've been in this industry, I've found the answer is almost always "to make money." A regular paycheck offers a sense of security many worry they will lose in retirement. Fortunately, we have a way to create the same sense of security so you can enjoy your retirement to the fullest. You can rest easy knowing, without fail, those paychecks are still on their way. As we move into the income planning section of our planning model, we'll be looking at the three main ways to generate income in retirement: Social Security, pensions, and investments. To start, let's discuss the best ways to maximize your Social Security benefits.

2
Income Planning Part 1

Maximizing Your Social Security Benefits

Have you heard the old saying, "You don't know what you don't know"? If you haven't, let me tell you a story to show you what I mean.

LeAnne and Andy had been married for forty-seven years. They shared a beautiful life together on an old family farm tucked away in a remote mountain area. The couple made their money through a variety of income sources, including selling produce, gathering forest debris for floral arrangements, running a fishery, and operating a Christmas tree farm. After struggling for many years, LeAnne decided to go back to college and earn her associate's degree in order to work at a local hospital. Shortly after, the couple sold the family farm and were able to purchase a nice single-family home near her new job.

As the years passed, Andy's health issues began to get the best of him. The time came for Andy to retire but, unfortunately, he did not have enough Social Security credits to qualify for benefits. With LeAnne now the sole breadwinner, the couple feared what the future might bring. LeAnne and Andy began to look for answers to deter a heart-wrenching future. They reached out to me for help.

This is where my understanding of the Social Security system came into play. The most satisfying part of my job is when I can step in and make a real difference in people's lives.

With our guidance, LeAnne and Andy found that once LeAnne turned on her Social Security benefit, Andy (who is three years older) could sign up for half of LeAnne's benefit. This would give them an additional $1,000 per month, more than enough to satisfy their spending plan. I mean, imagine what you could do with an extra $12,000 per year. That's quite a find!

Had this wonderful couple not sought the advice of a knowledgeable financial planner, they would have been facing financial struggles throughout the remainder of their lives. Now, this wonderful couple are able to finally enjoy their retirement worry free. My point is, sometimes you just don't know what you don't know. In order to get the information, it's best to seek out an expert. It can be tough to face gaps in our knowledge or ask for help; believe me, I know. But if you wait too long, those financial fears you are having just *may* become a reality.

Why is Social Security Important?

When it comes to understanding just how essential Social Security is, the numbers speak for themselves. Irena Dushi, an economist with the Social Security Administration, found half of all citizens ages sixty-five or older receive at least 50 percent of their family income from Social Security benefits. Not only that, but a quarter of this same demographic relies on Social Security benefits for 90 percent of their total income.[2] These statistics are precisely why I believe Social Security is one of the most pivotal pieces of legislation ever passed in the United States. So how did it begin?

After the disastrous stock market crash of 1929, the country was in turmoil. Unemployment rates had soared, poverty was rampant, and every day people were struggling to make ends meet. It was in this bleak landscape the Social Security Act of 1935 emerged.[3] Implemented as a part of President Franklin D. Roosevelt's "New Deal" plan, the Social Security Act was designed to give a lifeline to retirees. Another underlying motive for the

---

2   *The Importance of Social Security Benefits to the Income of the Aged Population.* (2017). Social Security Administration Research, Statistics, and Policy Analysis. https://www.ssa.gov/policy/docs/ssb/v77n2/v77n2p1.html
3   The United States Social Security Administration. (n.d.). *Social Security History.* Social Security Administration. https://www.ssa.gov/history/briefhistory3.html

program was to provide a vital source of income to keep millions of citizens out of the poor houses opened during the Great Depression. Social Security has continued to act as a safety net for Americans for over eighty-five years, improving their quality of life and allowing them to enjoy the retirement they have worked so hard to earn.

Despite the immense positive impact Social Security has had on so many hardworking Americans, this program is currently navigating through treacherous waters. The 2023 Trustees Report revealed some serious challenges the program is facing in the coming years, stating that without intervention, the Social Security Trust Fund will be depleted by 2034.[4] This means tens of millions of Americans will have their benefits cut anywhere between 20 percent and 25 percent. Let me paint a clearer picture of what this will look like with the following examples:

If Social Security Cuts are 20 percent:
- $1,500 per month becomes **$1,200 per month**
- $2,000 per month becomes **$1,600 per month**
- $2,500 per month becomes **$2,000 per month**
- $3,000 per month becomes **$2,400 per month**

Unfortunately, these cuts are only the beginning. Without some big changes, the program's long-term viability is in question. Now, this is not to say there aren't solutions. You

---

[4] The United States Social Security Administration. (2023). *Trustees Report summary*. Social Security Administration. https://www.ssa.gov/oact/trsum/

should plan both to have Social Security benefits *and* to maximize them during retirement. Still, I firmly believe we need to be aware of the challenges the program faces and the solutions to secure its future.

In order to fix this situation, I would encourage you to reach out to your congressional representative. The viability of Social Security is in jeopardy; if you want the program to be available to our grandchildren and the generations to follow, it's vital for Congress to take action immediately. Below, I've highlighted a few ways we can save Social Security. You can use these as a guide when you speak to your representative.

- **Payroll Tax Rate Increase:** Payroll taxes currently sit at a combined total of 12.4 percent, with half (6.2 percent) being paid by employers and half by employees. By raising this rate from 6.2 percent each to 6.5 percent each, we could fix a portion of the program's monetary shortfall. This means more revenue for the Social Security Trust Fund and more money to pay out those essential benefits.
- **Retirement Age Adjustment:** The Full Retirement Age (FRA) is currently between sixty-six and sixty-seven, depending on the year you were born. As life expectancies increase, it's only reasonable to think the FRA could also be bumped up a notch. By raising the FRA to

sixty-eight and gradually increasing it to seventy, we can ensure older retirees and benefit recipients have more financial security, but new recipients still have access to the benefits.
- **Raising the Income Cap:** The contribution and benefit base for Social Security is currently set at $160,200 (as of 2023), but any earnings above this cap are not subject to Social Security tax. Unfortunately, this limit restricts the program's revenue potential. If we raise this cap, we can provide the Social Security program with the financial stability it needs for the long haul.
- **Change the COLA Formula:** By modifying how Cost-of-Living Adjustments (COLA) are calculated, we could better account for inflation and lend a helping hand to those benefit recipients with lower incomes. These are the folks who rely on the program the most, and it's vital we ensure they can retire and StayRetired™.

This is just the beginning of the conversation. These problems should be on our radar, but right now we want to focus on something more immediate: understanding the rules of Social Security and finding the best ways to maximize your benefits. So on that note, let's keep moving forward.

Why is Maximizing Our Benefits Important?

One question many retirees ask themselves at one point or another is, "Will I have enough money to stay retired, or will I run out?" This is a valid concern, and it's rooted in the concept of longevity or the potentially long duration of an individual's life. This sounds like a good thing, right? Well, when it comes to finances, a long life could mean you outlive your hard-earned money.

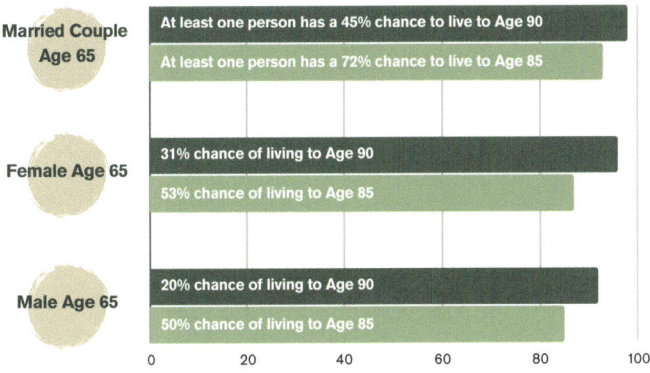

Why should you plan to live a long life? Because you might live a long life. *Let me repeat this in a different way. You need to plan to live a long life, because you might!* If you don't, then your financial worries are officially over. But when we are talking about income planning, especially Social Security planning, we must address and account for the risk of longevity. The first step to doing so is to understand what rules you need to follow to maximize one of your biggest sources of retirement income: Social Security benefits.

Understanding the Full Retirement Age (FRA)

One of the most crucial factors you need to grasp before filing for Social Security is your FRA and the impacts of collecting benefits too early.

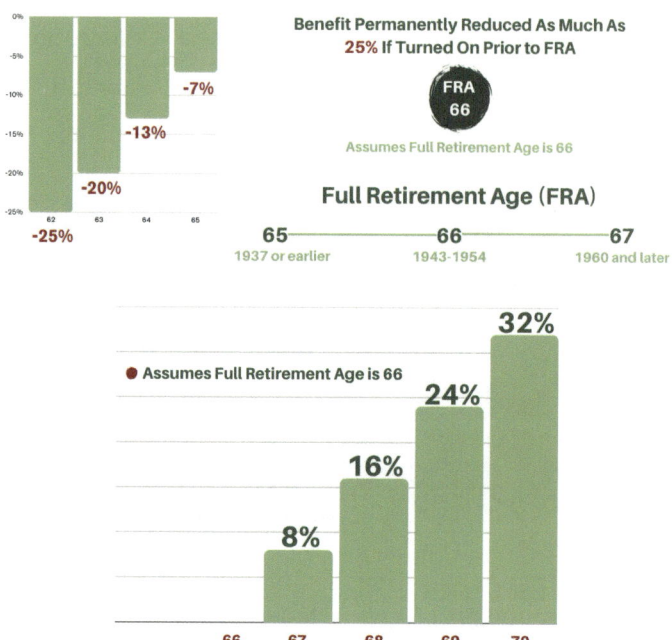

Suppose your FRA is sixty-six and you're eager to get those benefits flowing before then. Well, here's the harsh truth: You may face a benefit reduction as high as 25 percent. You might be saying "Well, I heard the reduction isn't permanent!" I can tell you, this is absolutely fake news. Once you turn your benefits on, they're locked in, and the reduction is **permanent**. (Note: There is a one-time provision to withdraw. As stated on SSA.gov,

"If you change your mind about receiving benefits, you may be able to withdraw your Social Security claim if it has been less than twelve months since you were first entitled to benefits. To withdraw your claim, you must meet all the requirements, including making the request in writing and repaying the benefits you received. If you withdraw your claim, you may reapply at a future date." It is rare someone takes advantage of this option.)

Don't get me wrong; you still have many options at your disposal. There are ninety-five different opportunities to turn on your benefits between the ages of sixty-two and seventy, one for each month between those ages (though it's important to remember, you cannot collect until you are one month past your sixty-second birthday). If you are part of a married couple, your opportunities increase dramatically with a whopping 500 separate times you can turn on your combined benefits. This is part of what makes Social Security planning so complex, and getting this timing right is essential.

Here's the exciting part: Every month you wait, the benefit is going to increase a little bit. And once you reach your FRA, your Primary Insurance Amount (PIA) will be calculated. Of course, PIA is just fancy lingo for the amount you'll receive from Social Security at your FRA. So, what's the best way to maximize these benefits? Simple: **Wait until the age of seventy to collect.** By waiting, you'll be able to snag the maximum benefit. But, and this is important, you need to consult with your financial planner to see if this aligns with your assets and income stream. Waiting until seventy might be a smart move for some, while others might find it better to collect at sixty-two. When someone asks me when they should turn on their Social Security benefit, my initial response is always, "It depends." Actually, it depends on a lot of factors, all of which can be addressed inside a good StayRetired™ Financial Plan.

Another trick of the trade you may not know about is the incentive the Social Security program offers for those who can hold off benefit collection. Each year you delay collection beyond your FRA, you'll get what is known as Delayed Retirement Credits. As of 2023, these credits boost your benefits by a cool 8 percent per year.[5] That's roughly two-thirds of a percentage point each month, adding up to a potential 32 percent increase. The increase from sixty-two to sixty-six is 25 percent. Added to the 32 percent from FRA to age seventy and you can pick up a cool 57 percent by waiting to start collecting your benefit. So, if you wait until seventy instead of sixty-two, it's nearly 57 percent more in monthly benefits (in addition to cost-of-living adjustments added annually). Over your lifetime, this could be a difference of $100,000 or more in benefits. If you ask me, that's just too much money to

---

5 "What Are Delayed Retirement Credits for Social Security?" (2023, February 7). AARP. https://www.aarp.org/retirement/social-security/questions-answers/delayed-retirement-credits.html

risk leaving on the table because you didn't understand the rules of the system.

Can You Work and Collect Social Security?

The short answer is yes, but this is generally where folks get into a tricky situation, especially when it comes to benefit repayment. Let's look at three ways this scenario could play out.

1. **After Reaching Your FRA:** Once you reach your FRA, you're in the clear. You can keep working, collect your SS benefits, and receive the full amount without needing to repay a single dime. That's not to say you may not be subject to income taxes, but we'll talk more about that later.
2. **The Year You Reach Your FRA:** This is where some limits come into play. If you decide to apply for benefits the year you turn your FRA, there will be an income limit to consider. For 2024, the limit is set at $59,520 a year or $4,960 a month. For every three dollars your income exceeds this limit, you'll have to repay one dollar back of your Social Security benefits. (Thankfully, this limit is adjusted annually for inflation.)
3. **Before Reaching Your FRA:** If you choose to collect benefits before reaching your FRA, the income limit is even smaller. In 2024, it's set at $22,320 per year or $1860 per month. (Again, if

you are reading this past 2024, the good news is this number typically increases each year due to inflation.) As with the second scenario, there's a bit of give-and-take. In this scenario, for every two dollars you earn above that limit, you'll have to repay one dollar of your Social Security benefits.

So why is there benefit repayment at all? Well, it's the government's way of saying, "We want you to be retired when you start collecting." Social Security wasn't originally intended as a "continue to work and collect" type of program, so while you *can* do this, you'll have to pay up. Keep in mind pensions and annuities won't be factored in here; only income coming from W-2 or 1099 earnings. The right financial planner can help you structure your income streams so you can avoid this benefit repayment, but we'll talk more about that later.

Here's an example to help put benefit repayment in perspective. Assume Mary started collecting her Social Security benefits on January 1, 2024, and the benefit was $1,800. She plans to work throughout the year and expects to earn $32,320. How much did Mary earn above the income limit? In this case, $10,000 of her income will be above the $22,320 cap. If the penalty is two dollars for every one dollar earned, then she will have to pay back $5,000 of her Social Security benefits. Since Mary's benefit was $1,800 per month, in order for the Social Security Administration (SSA) to recover the penalty amount, Mary will not receive Social Security for the first three months of *the following year* until the penalty is satisfied. If Mary had waited to collect her benefits, she could have avoided these penalties. That's why, in my opinion, and notwithstanding your financial situation, it's almost always better to wait and allow those benefits to grow until you have fully retired and stopped working.

Social Security Taxes

Let's shift gears and talk about taxes, **specifically income taxes**. Social Security benefits are not taxable *unless there is other income.*

Let me say it another way: If Social Security is your only income, it is not subject to income tax. But when other income is introduced, up to 85 percent of Social Security can be subject to income taxes. What if I told you I could show you a way to pay zero taxes on your Social Security benefits? It may sound too good to be true, but it's entirely possible.

The key is to make Social Security **your only source of income**. Now I know it isn't always so simple, and you may have other income streams to deal with. Even then, there are ways to significantly reduce your tax liability. The goal of any good retirement plan should be to pay as little income taxes as possible, and with Social Security benefits, we have ways to work a bit of magic.

To show you the way we do this, let's look at two separate couples.

First, we have Mark and Brenda. They decide to apply for their benefits early. To satisfy their spending plan and cover their expenses, they need a total annual income of $78,872. Their Social Security benefits provide $24,000 per year, so they'll have to withdraw $54,872 from their IRA to cover the remaining expenses and potential tax liabilities for the year. However, since they are withdrawing a large amount from their IRA, a large portion of their Social Security benefits becomes taxable. By restructuring their income and utilizing their Social Security benefits more efficiently, they could potentially significantly lower their overall tax liability. We can see this in action with our next couple.

Mark & Brenda: Applied Early for Social Security

Section 1	Enter Here ↓	Page 2, 1040		Original
Wages, Salaries, Tips		1	→	0
Tax-Exempt Interest		2a	0	
Interest Income		2b	→	0
Qualified Dividends		3a	0	
Ordinary Dividends		3b	→	0
Gross IRA Distributions		4a	54,617	
Taxable IRAs		4b	→	54,617
Gross Pensions		5a	0	
Taxable Pensions		5b	→	0
Gross Social Security		6a	24,000	24,000
Taxable S.S.		6b	85%	20,400

Mark & Brenda: Applied Early for Social Security

Section 2	Breakdown of Taxes			
Tax Year	2023	2023		
Taxes	Original	Revised	Rev $ Diff	% Changed
Pg 2, Ln 16	4,878	5,120	0	0%
AMT, Sch 2,L1	0	0	0	
NIT, Sch 2,L8	0	0	0	
Federal	4,878	5,120	0	0%
State	1,739	1,752	0	5.3%
Taxes	Original	Revised	Rev $ Diff	% Changed
Total Tax	**6,617**	**6,617**	**0**	**0%**

Section 3	
$24,000	Social Security
$54,617	IRA
$78,617	Total
$75,017	Taxable
$30,700	Std. Ded.
$44,317	Taxable
12%	(Top Tax Bracket)
$4,878	Federal Tax
$1,739	NC State Tax
$6,617	Total Tax
After-Tax Income	
$72,000/year	
$6,000/month	

John & Connie:
Used Strategy to Apply for Social Security

Section 1	Enter Here ↓	Page 1, 1040		Original
Wages, Salaries, Tips		1	→	
Tax-Exempt Interest		2a	0	
Interest Income		2b	→	
Qualified Dividends		3a	0	
Ordinary Dividends		3b	→	
Gross IRA Distributions		4a	20,000	
Taxable IRAs		4b	→	**20,000**
Gross Pensions		5a	0	
Taxable Pensions		5b	→	
Gross Social Security		6a	52,000	52,000
Taxable S.S.		6b	15%	7,700

John and Connie need $72,000 to cover their yearly expenses; $52,000 of it is going to come from their Social Security benefits, making it their primary source of income. Since Social Security is a majority of their income, they only need to withdraw $20,000 from their IRA to meet their financial goal. This would effectively put them in a zero percent tax bracket. (Because Social Security is not taxable and the IRA falls below the taxable threshold, they are in a zero dollar tax bracket that year.)

It's important to remember that individual tax situations vary, and tax rates are subject to change.

John & Connie:
Used Strategy to Apply for Social Security

Section 2	Breakdown of Taxes			
Tax Year	2023	2023		
Taxes	Original	Revised	Rev $ Diff	% Changed
Pg 2, Ln 16	0	0	0	0%
AMT, Sch 2,L1	0	0	0	
NIT, Sch 2,L8	0	0	0	
Federal	0	0	0	0%
State	0	0	0	5.3%
Taxes	Original	Revised	Rev $ Diff	% Changed
Total Tax	**0**	**0**	**0**	**0%**

Section 3	
$20,000	Social Security
$52,000	IRA
$72,000	Total
$27,700	Taxable
$29,121	Std. Ded.
$-1,421	Taxable
0%	Tax Bracket
After-Tax Income	
$72,000/year	
$6,000/month	

Maximizing your benefits and minimizing your tax liability is a complex process, and it requires careful planning and consideration of your income sources, retirement accounts, and overall tax strategy. Working with a knowledgeable financial or retirement planner can help you navigate these complexities and develop a plan to fit your unique financial goals.

How Do Spousal Benefits Work?

When it comes to spousal benefits, many of the rules in place are designed to help provide support to the lower-earning spouse. This spouse is entitled to the greater of either their own benefit or 50 percent of the higher earning spouse's benefit. Just like with a traditional benefits claim, you can start getting these benefits one month after your sixty-second birthday. Just keep in mind, grabbing them too early can trigger a reduction. So it may be best to hold off as long as you can to squeeze out the maximum benefits.

In addition to spousal benefits, there are widow's benefits. It's not a pleasant subject to discuss, but if you find yourself in the unfortunate position of losing your spouse, Social Security has your back. Starting at the age of sixty, you can receive a widow's benefit. According to Joe Elsasser, who runs a firm called Covisum specializing in explaining Social Security benefits, you can receive the amount your departed spouse was receiving or entitled to receive. Under certain situations, you may be able to collect this benefit and still allow your own benefit to grow and then switch to it later, if it is higher. Here's the kicker: If you have just become a widow, now would be a good time to engage with a knowledgeable financial advisor who can help you navigate Social Security and the additional financial changes you could be forced to navigate alone.

How to Stay Up to Date on Social Security

Keeping up with all the changes in the Social Security program can be a real challenge. Believe me, I've been at it for years. One of my go-to resources is the Old-Age, Survivors and Disability Insurance (OASDI) Trustees Report. Each year, I dig into this report to find out all the latest developments in the world of Social Security. I also received my CSSCS (Certification in Social Security Claiming Strategies) and a certification from the NSSA (National Social Security Association).[6] Let me tell you, getting these certifications wasn't a walk in the park. If you really want to get certified and know the ins and outs of Social Security, you'll have to dedicate a lot of time and effort to acquiring them. I understand not everyone wants to go through all the trouble, which is why I recommend just getting a financial planner with extensive knowledge of the Social Security system. They can save you time and money by untangling the intricate web of Social Security and guiding you to make the right decisions regarding your benefits.

---

6   Designations indicated do not constitute an endorsement or approval of any government agency.

Social Security Isn't the Only Form of Income You Can Have in Retirement

While Social Security benefits can be a significant contributor to your retirement income, you probably don't want to rely just on Social Security alone. I am sure you've heard the saying "Don't put all your eggs in one basket." This definitely applies to income planning. In part two of our income planning section, we're going to dive into the world of pensions and annuities. I'll break these financial instruments down for you, explain exactly how they work, and show you how to get the most out of these income streams in retirement.

3
Income Planning Part 2
Pensions 101 and the Rise of the 401(k) Plan

While Social Security benefits are important, there has traditionally been another foundational pillar of retirement income: *pensions*. Well before the creation of Social Security in 1935, pensions acted as a way for companies to honor their loyal employees, symbolizing their gratitude for decades of service. Back in those days, it was common for folks to dedicate their entire careers to one company; they'd work for thirty years, receive a gold watch, and enjoy a comfortable pension in their golden years. This wasn't limited to specific industries. Government employees and union members were commonly given pension plans as well.

As the landscape of retirement savings continued to evolve, traditional pension plans became growing financial liabilities for companies. These businesses realized they could be supporting retirees for several decades. While industry leaders looked for alternatives, a significant retirement savings shift was about to occur.

The Birth of the 401(k) Plan

Fast forward to the late 1970s and the passage of the Revenue Act of 1978. This act not only brought about changes in tax rates but introduced a provision that would revolutionize retirement savings. The potential of this provision, which added section 401(k) to the Internal Revenue Code, would be seen by the man you see me standing with above, renowned financial professional Ted Benna.

Joe Roseman and Ted Banna

Ted might not resemble a former linebacker for the Dallas Cowboys, but he had a keen eye for finances. Through his interpretation of the Revenue Act, he found a way for employees to save a portion of their pretax salary and receive a matching contribution from their employers. Excited about his discovery, Ted approached several companies to share his 401(k)-plan concept, but they were skeptical. "We don't think this is possible, Ted. Sorry, but you're wrong." So, what did Ted do? He said, "No problem, I'll just do it myself!" Ted decided to use the strategy in his own company's retirement plan, and before long, numerous companies were doing the exact same thing. By the early 1980s, the adoption of 401(k) plans was skyrocketing.

The original intent of these plans was to give employees more control over their retirement savings. Unlike traditional pension plans, which bound employees to a specific company, 401(k) plans offered something new: portability. This meant people could take their money with them if they decided to switch jobs. This newfound flexibility allowed individuals to manage their retirement funds in previously unimaginable ways, opening up doors that allowed millions to explore additional savings opportunities. Sadly, as with numerous innovations, there have been unintended consequences.

Traditional Pension Plans Have Begun to Vanish

Companies began to recognize just how much financial liability they had when it came to traditional pension plans. These companies started to think, "If this guy retires and lives another thirty years, we'll be on the hook for that pension for decades!" That's when they discovered the magic of 401(k) matching and other alternatives. These options drastically reduced their long-term financial obligations. Nowadays, you'll only find a handful of Fortune 500 companies still using a traditional pension plan.

Even if you do have a pension, it's possible for the plans to collapse. I've had several clients who worked for the airlines; they once had some of the most robust pensions around. But even those plans began to take a nosedive, which is where the Pension Benefit Guaranty Corporation (PBGC) came in. The government formed the PBGC to ensure that individuals still received partial benefits if their pension plans went under. Despite the presence of the PBGC, there remains a risk of leaving your funds within the pension system. Let me tell you the story of a few clients who encountered this problem.

My clients, Sarah and John, worked for a major airline: Sarah as a flight attendant and John as a mid-level manager. With twenty-five years of service under their belts, their pension benefits looked promising. It was projected for Sarah to receive $2,500 a month and John would receive $3,000 a month. Unfortunately, the pension plan began to crumble, and the PBGC had to step in. Their benefits were slashed, with Sarah's reduced to $900 (originally $2,500 a month) and John's to $700 (originally $3,000 a month). While it could have been worse, this serves as a cautionary tale. Sometimes, it's better to consider other options besides a pension.

Modern Alternatives: Cash Balance Plans

In addition to 401(k) plans, some companies transitioned from traditional pensions to more modern alternatives like the *cash balance plan*. These plans kept the core concept of a pension, giving employees a benefit they could use in retirement. However, there was a twist: In a cash balance plan, each employee has an individual account where the employer contributes a percentage of their salary annually. This creates a pool of money growing over time, similar to a personal savings account.

The beauty of the cash balance plan lies in its flexibility. You can opt for a lump sum payment and transfer money to other retirement instruments. Alternatively, you can convert the balance into an annuity. These options give you more control over your retirement savings. It's the best of both worlds: the security of a pension-like benefit combined with the flexibility of other retirement options. Plus, it can be a bit less risky than a 401(k) plan. Nice bonus, right?

Speaking of 401(k) plans, let's talk about their associated risks. Remember we discussed longevity risk earlier, which is simply the fear of outliving your money? Well, with a traditional pension, it's not a problem. The company guarantees to pay you a certain amount of dollars for the rest of your life. They take care of managing the investment, so as long as you're alive, you'll receive that payout. But with a 401(k), the responsibility for the payout and investment performance rests on the individual. It takes a significant financial burden off the company's shoulders.

If you are fortunate enough to have a pension, you may be wondering how to take advantage of it. Many traditional pension plans come with their own distinct set of considerations and implications. It's essential to understand these completely in order to get the most out of this income source.

I Have a Pension; How Do I Take It?

If you do have a pension, the first thing you'll want to do is familiarize yourself with the options offered by your company. The first option many traditional pension plans offer is *single life*; by choosing this plan you are essentially saying, "I want a steady stream of income for as long as I'm alive." While single life plans almost always have the highest payout, there is one thing to consider if you choose this path. If the unexpected happens and you depart this world prematurely, the remaining balance of your pension evaporates into thin air (or, more specifically, back into the company's coffers).

Sadly, this means your loved ones won't have access to those funds. We can't pull off any *Weekend at Bernie's* schemes to change that reality. Instead, they will only be left with what you received during your lifetime. Fortunately, many companies include additional options to provide a guaranteed payout for a specific period, usually a minimum of ten years. This way, you can choose between a lifetime stream of income or a fixed payment for a set duration.

Another option to consider is *joint life*. This plan allows you and your spouse to reap the benefits of your pension throughout your retirement. Within the joint life option, there are a few variations to explore, including:

- **Joint Life with 100 Percent to Both Spouses:** In this scenario, full pension payments continue as long as either spouse is alive. It provides a safety net for both partners, ensuring their financial stability.
- **Joint Life with 75 Percent to Surviving Spouse:** Should one spouse pass away, the surviving partner will receive 75 percent of the pension benefits until their passing. This provision still offers substantial financial support to the surviving spouse.
- **Joint Life with 50 Percent to Surviving Spouse:** With this option, if one spouse passes away, the surviving partner continues to receive 50 percent of the pension benefits. While it's a slightly reduced amount, it still provides ongoing income. This option, coupled with the correct amount of life insurance, could provide an even larger benefit to the surviving spouse than even the Joint Life with 100 Percent to Both Spouses.

Keep in mind that the world of pension plans is vast, with numerous variations and percentages to consider. We won't delve into all the details here, as this isn't a dissertation on pensions. Still, our objective as fiduciaries is to ensure that the best option is utilized when it comes to income planning. Remember, the *key* is to find the approach aligning with your unique circumstances and goals. This is where expert guidance and a comprehensive StayRetired™ Financial Plan can make all the difference.

Sometimes leaving the pension with the company is the optimal choice, but in many cases, taking the cash balance and creating your own private pension can be advantageous. This approach involves transferring the cash balance to a private annuity. The result would be to create lifetime benefits for both spouses, in addition to ensuring if there were a premature death, the heirs would receive the proceeds of the annuity. This strategy helps create a win for both the retiree, their spouse, and potentially their children or other heirs.

How to Maximize Your Income by Creating a Private Pension

Creating a private pension involves leveraging annuity lifetime benefits to enhance your income during retirement. When crafting these pensions, we take several crucial elements into account that can influence your financial situation. By comprehensively analyzing these factors, we can devise a tailored plan to maximize your income in retirement.

These factors include:
- Social Security
- Company pensions
- Government pensions
- Available income streams from other investments
- Income streams from real estate or rental properties

The initial decision is to choose how to receive the cash balance plan or pension. You'll also need to decide whether you'll choose a lump sum or annuity. Typically, with government or union pensions, you may have limited options or you may be required to accept what the pension company offers. In those situations, I engage my clients in a thorough discussion about their spending plan and retirement goals. Together, we select the most suitable option based on their specific circumstances.

If the option of choosing a lump sum is available, this means you would receive the entire accumulated pension funds at once, allowing you to invest the funds according to your preference. One drawback is that if you perform this step incorrectly, you could reintroduce the longevity risk back into the mix because you would be forced to manage your funds to ensure they last throughout your retirement. On the other hand, if the funds were transferred into a private annuity, this instrument could be structured to provide a guaranteed lifetime income stream, effectively addressing the longevity risk associated with retirement. (**Caution:** *If you handle this step incorrectly, you could trigger income taxes or a penalty of the proceeds.*)

In numerous cases we have encountered, a viable option was to transfer the cash balance and put it somewhere else. If the goal is to create guaranteed lifetime income to mirror or enhance the pension component, we would explore the products provided by insurance companies because they specialize in measuring this specific type of risk. The goal of this entire exercise is to design a "private" pension to provide you with a dependable income stream for your entire life, which transforms longevity from a risk into a rewarding aspect of your retirement.

The most significant difference between a traditional pension plan and a private annuity plan lies in what happens if you die prematurely. With a private annuity plan, funded through a life insurance company annuity, any remaining funds in your annuity will be directly transferred to your beneficiaries, ensuring they receive the benefit at your death. By integrating a private annuity plan, you can guarantee a lifelong income for you and your spouse, for life. The bottom line is if you leave the money and take distribution from a traditional pension plan and *you die too soon*, you risk your heirs getting nothing.

Understanding the Different Types of Annuities: Pros, Cons, and How They Fit into Your StayRetired™ Financial Plan

Annuities may seem like a new concept, but they've actually been around for ages. The first annuities can be traced back to ancient Egypt, but it was the Romans who firmly established the concept. Annuities today operate by providing a lump sum of money to an insurance company, which in turn guarantees specific benefits. But here's the thing: Annuities have become a bit controversial. There's a lot of information out there—some good, some bad, and some downright ugly. But it's important to remember a lot of the negative stuff you hear about annuities comes straight from the large Wall Street investment firms that are in competition with insurance companies. Why? Because they can't make money off managing your money if you have taken the funds away from them and placed them in an annuity, and these companies hate it when they're not making a profit! So, let's put negativity aside and focus on the different types of annuities and how they can fit into your income plan.

Annuity Type #1: Variable
- **Pros:**
  - Moderate growth potential
  - Tax-deferred
- **Cons:**
  - High cost
  - Lack of principal protection

- Exposure to market volatility and risk
- Potential surrender fees

Variable annuities tie your contract's growth directly to the stock market. Your money is invested in a separate account, which is much like a mutual fund. This means the annuity's performance increases or decreases with the market. If you're seeking substantial growth potential within your annuity, this might be the ticket for you. But there are a few things to keep in mind. First, variable annuities don't give you protection on your principal investment. Just like stocks and bonds, the annuity's account balance within the annuity will fluctuate as the market moves. Another downside is the cost. Variable annuities tend to be expensive. By looking at the industry data, we can see the internal costs range from 3.5 percent to 5.75 percent of the total investment. "Because of the lack of principal protection and the fee structure, variable annuities are not the best for the risk averse."[7] There are other instruments available that do have principal protection and have much lower costs or, in some cases, no fees involved. We will discuss those next.

---

7   J.B. Maverick, "What Is a Good Expense Ratio for Mutual Funds?" Investopedia. (2021, April 20). https://www.investopedia.com/ask/answers/032715/when-expense-ratio-considered-high-and-when-it-considered-low.asp, Accessed 2/18/22.

Annuity Type #2: Fixed

- **Pros:**
  - Guaranteed income for a specific period
  - Principle protection
- **Cons:**
  - Limited growth potential
  - Fails to provide adequate protection against inflation
  - Potential surrender fees

Next up, we have fixed annuities. Because of the recent rise in interest rates, these have become more popular lately. The significant advantage of choosing a fixed annuity is the certainty it offers. You know precisely what the growth rate will be, and your principal is protected. With fixed annuities, you get a straightforward option offering stability. Of course, there are limits. For example, fixed annuities don't offer much in the way of inflation protection. If inflation rates are high, the rates of your fixed annuity likely won't keep pace. So, suppose inflation is at 10 percent and your annuity yields 5 percent; you're still down 5 percent in purchasing power. It's not as bad as the losses you would experience with a variable annuity, which would feel the heat both from inflation and a stock market drop. Because of this, fixed annuities have the potential to be an attractive option.

Annuity Type #3: Fixed Index
- **Pros:**
  - Growth potential
  - Tax-deferred
  - Guaranteed income options
  - Hedges against inflation
  - Principal protection
- **Cons:**
  - Highly complex
  - No growth = no credit
  - Potential surrender fees

In my seminars, I like to ask the audience a question: "Does anyone here have children or grandchildren who are smarter than they are?" The fixed index annuity is like the smart child or grandchild! A fixed index annuity uses specific indexes whose returns are measured by the index they are tied to, many of which are uncapped. This means in the fixed index annuity you could be seeing returns comparable to the returns in variable annuities. But unlike the stock market, fixed index annuities are a fixed product, and your principal is protected. So even if the stock market goes down, your $100,000 in a fixed index annuity would still be $100,000. Another advantage is that you can guarantee income for yourself (or you and your spouse).[8] This is the private annuity

---

8   When lifetime income is guaranteed, typically there is a fee charged for that guarantee. Guarantees are backed by the financial strength and claims paying ability of the issuing company.

option we discussed earlier in detail. Of course, there is a downside. If there's no index growth, there's no credit. But in stock market instruments, that "no credit" would typically be a loss. At the same time, there would be no loss due to stock market concerns.

Safeguarding Your Wealth

You've worked hard to secure your retirement income, but it's equally important to protect and grow your wealth. Making informed investment decisions and implementing effective asset protection strategies are key to ensuring the long-term security of your finances. In the next chapter, we will delve into the best practices for safeguarding your wealth, provide you with valuable insights, and introduce a powerful tool we use to assess and manage investment risks.

4
Asset Protection and Investment Planning

Cash, Income and Growth

When it comes to managing assets and making intelligent investment decisions, one name always comes to mind: Warren Buffet. Buffet is known for many things, but primarily for his immense wealth, vast business knowledge, and remarkable investment success. However, he's also known for his unique approach to life, even the way he eats breakfast.

Now, that may sound strange, but stick with me here. Warren Buffet, the Oracle of Omaha, has a fascinating habit when it comes to his first meal of the day. In a candid interview,[9] he revealed a morning ritual reflecting his keen

---

9 K. Elkins. (2018, April 18). "Warren Buffett Eats the Same Thing for Breakfast

awareness of his financial well-being. As he shaves in the morning, he asks his wife to leave a specific amount of money in a cup for his morning meal, either $2.61, $2.95, or $3.17. Each amount corresponds to one of his three go-to breakfast items, reflecting his outlook on the market and his current financial mood.

"When I'm not feeling quite so prosperous, I might go with the $2.61, which is two sausage patties, and then I put them together and pour myself a Coke. $3.17 is a bacon, egg, and cheese biscuit, but the market's down this morning, so I'll pass up the $3.17 and go with the $2.95," Buffet explained in the HBO documentary, *Becoming Warren Buffet*.

Now you might be saying, "What on earth does Warren Buffet's breakfast ritual have to do with protecting your wealth and planning your investments?" Well, it's not about the meal itself, but the mindset behind it. Warren's morning routine perfectly illustrates his disciplined and pragmatic approach to financial decision-making.

By associating the price of his breakfast with the market's performance, Warren showcases the importance of maintaining a clear-headed perspective when it comes to managing wealth. He recognizes that the market fluctuates and that economic conditions can impact one's financial well-being. His morning ritual serves as a reminder that financial decisions, even as seemingly

---

Every Day—and It Never Costs More Than $3.17." *CNBC*. https://www.cnbc.com/2018/04/18/warren-buffett-buys-breakfast-from-mcdonalds-for-under-3-point-17.html

trivial as a breakfast sandwich, should be made with thoughtful consideration of the bigger picture.

Just as Warren Buffet's breakfast ritual reminds us of the importance of keeping an eye on our assets, it also emphasizes the significance of strategic financial planning. To protect your assets and plan your investments to their full potential, you'll want to understand the role of the three main planning categories: **cash**, **income**, and **growth**.

Three Primary StayRetired™ Planning Buckets: Cash, Income, and Growth

To make our process easy to understand, we like to separate the planning categories into three "buckets" to hold your assets. The first two are primarily designed to deal with incidental costs and expenses outlined in your spending plan, while the third is all about increasing your total net worth and retirement funds. Let's start with your first line of defense against emergencies: cash.

Bucket #1: Cash

Step #1
You must have a Separate Bucket of Liquid Cash for Expected and Unexpected Emergencies.

Life is unpredictable, and unfortunately, retirement is no exception. There you are, sailing through the vast ocean of retirement. You're happy, smiling in the sunshine, sipping on a margarita. Then, off the bow of your ship, you start to see storm clouds gather on the horizon. Now this may run some folks aground, but if you have liquid cash on hand, it can act as a vital lifeline. It means you can keep sailing and, more importantly, **Stay Retired™**!

This is why we recommend all of our clients have an emergency fund to deal with those unexpected events. Whether it's a surprise medical expense, unforeseen home repair, or a sudden market downturn, having cash on hand ensures you protect your assets and won't have to tap into your investments or benefits at the wrong time. This money can function as a safety net, giving you a sense of security that will allow you to enjoy retirement stress-free.

Bucket #2: Income

Step #2
Create Retirement Income that is dependable and has the potential to increase over time.

When it comes to your income bucket, it's crucial to ensure a steady flow of money. As we discussed in previous chapters, income can be derived from a range of sources such as Social Security benefits, pensions, and annuities. These income streams form the backbone of your financial plan, providing a consistent and reliable source of funds to satisfy your spending plan.

The key to optimizing your income bucket lies in *careful* structuring and strategic decision-making. This means understanding the intricacies of Social Security, researching your pensions, and utilizing your annuities to their full potential. For example, exploring strategies such as timing your Social Security benefits to maximize your monthly payments or selecting the most beneficial pension payout options can significantly impact your overall retirement income.

But it's not just about generating income—it's about making your money work for you. By employing effective investment strategies, you can potentially enhance your returns and create opportunities for growth, which brings us to our final bucket.

Bucket #3: Growth (a.k.a. Investment and Recovery)

Step #3
A Method To Invest, Grow, Replenish and Recover Your Principal WITHOUT Excessive Risk

In addition to his eccentric breakfast practices, Warren Buffet has a number of insights about growing investments. One of his quotes I've always enjoyed is, "If you don't find a way to make money while you sleep, you will work until you die." What this means is, basically, you'll want a portion of your retirement nest egg in the stock market for the long term, as this can exponentially grow your wealth. Now, this isn't always easy. Growth requires patience, resilience, and a long-term perspective. We're not talking about quick wins or overnight successes here—you need to be in it for the long haul.

The core of our investment philosophy lies in the power of the market. Therefore, a measured portion of your investment bucket will find its home in the dynamic realm of the stock market. While we can't give you specific recommendations in this book, we can help guide you to an overall potentially profitable investment strategy. Here are some of the investment instruments that may come into play:

- **Stocks:** Individual shares in a specific company can offer massive growth and capital appreciation opportunities, potentially skyrocketing your portfolio's success. Of course, individual stocks can present a significant amount of risk, so you'll need to choose which tickers you invest in carefully.
- **ETFs (Exchange-Traded Funds):** For a taste of stocks, consider utilizing ETFs. These versatile investment vehicles provide diversification and flexibility, allowing you to gain exposure to a basket of securities within a specific sector or index without the potential higher volatility of individual stocks.
- **Real Estate:** There is no shortage of ways to use real estate in your investment portfolio. From residential properties to commercial spaces and real estate investment trusts (also known as REITs), the real estate market presents avenues for income generation and long-term appreciation.
- **Annuities:** We covered this subject in chapter 3, but to recap, annuities are insurance-based financial products combining the benefits of guaranteed income and growth potential. In the context of investments, certain types of annuities

include uncapped strategies to capture indexed market gains. Once the gains have been captured at the end of each one-year or two-year period, these gains are locked in and are not subject to subsequent market downturns. Properly structured, these instruments can provide a steady way to grow your assets.

There is potential in the stock market, and the opportunities are ripe for those who are willing to sow the seeds of their hard-earned capital. Of course, the market isn't without its risks. There will be ups and downs, twists and turns, bear markets, and bull markets. But when my clients voice their fears about investment turbulence, I always tell them to take a step back. The stock market has a historical pattern of growth and upward movement, and more often than not, it will reward patient and steadfast investors.

In our growth bucket, also known as our investment and recovery bucket, the aim is to harness the power of this upward trajectory while preserving your hard-earned money. Together, we can embark on a calculated journey, picking a length of time during which we seek to grow and replenish your original principal investment. It's like tending to a delicate plant, providing it with the nourishment and care it needs to thrive. While we can't get into specific recommendations or percentages, we can help you embark on a calculated journey to align your goals and risk tolerance, where the desired outcome is

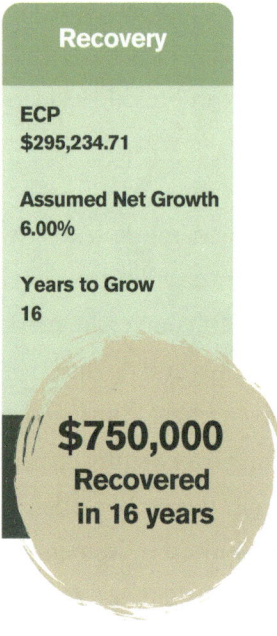

Investment Recovery
$295,234.71

Recovery
ECP $295,234.71
Assumed Net Growth 6.00%
Years to Grow 16

$750,000 Recovered in 16 years

to allow your wealth to grow and multiply.

Growth requires a delicate balance, and just like caring for a garden, you must prune, trim, and occasionally make adjustments to ensure optimal growth and prevent excessive risks. This is why our investment strategies adjust as specific conditions change in order to seize opportunities and weather difficult storms. A good strategy can also be essential when it comes to investment recovery. To show how this would work in real life, let's look at an example.

Case Study: Tim and Betty Johnson

Cash	Income
Additional Needs	Income
$50,000.00	$404,765.29

Additional Needs	Leg 1	Leg 2
ECP $50,000.00	Starting Principal $175,000.00	Starting Principal $229,765.29
	Owner	Owner
Est. Roth Conversion	Begins in Year 2023	Begins in Year 2028
Taxes $0.00	Bonus	Bonus

A couple of years ago, the Johnsons approached us for guidance on how to balance their cash, income, and investments. Tim, a sprightly sixty-five-year-old, was eagerly awaiting his retirement the following year, while Betty had already entered retirement at the age of sixty-four. With a portfolio of investable assets amounting to $750,000, their financial journey presented both opportunities and challenges. Their income needs and spending plan were clear: They needed roughly $7,000 per month to support their desired lifestyle. To ensure their retirement was built on a solid foundation, we set aside $50,000 as a cushion of cash reserves; this functioned as a safety net for unexpected expenses.

As for the income portion of their plan, they required $6,850 per month to cover their expenses. Betty's Social Security contributed $2,100, while Tim's added $2,800. Additionally, Tim enjoyed a company pension of $1,050. Altogether, their monthly income amounted to $5,950, leaving a shortfall of $1,000 per month. To bridge this gap, we strategically allocated $175,000 to generate an additional $1,034 per month once they commenced their retirement plan.

In these cases, it's also essential to look to the future. We've all seen the rough effects of inflation recently, so it's important to prepare. To help the Johnsons fight inflation, we designed a second leg allocating $229,000 as a means to generate income after a five-year wait. Looking ahead, we envision an additional $1,629 per month entering their pockets representing a remarkable 23 percent increase in their income. Overall, Tim and Betty's story is a testament to the power of strategic planning and the profound impact it can have on securing a prosperous retirement.

Risk Assessment

Before any investment decisions or recommendations are made, we always start by assessing risk tolerance. To streamline this process, the client responds to a Risk Tolerance Questionnaire. Once we have the score, we can compare it to industry analysis and make adjustments until the portfolio matches the risk tolerance. This allows us to measure just how much money our clients can invest in the future and still meet their personal risk tolerance.

The Risk Tolerance Questionnaire consists of nine questions. Once completed, we rank the score between zero and thirty, with zero being the lowest amount of risk tolerance and thirty being the highest.

Risk Tolerance Questionnaire

Question #1: What type of returns are you seeking?
1. Income
2. Growth greater than inflation
3. Maximum growth potential

Question #2: How long will it be before you intend to use the funds involved with this investment?
1. Immediately

2. Within five years
3. Five to ten years
4. Ten to twenty years

Question #3: Which best describes your expected future earnings over the next five years?
1. Stay constant
2. Keep pace with inflation
3. Stay ahead of inflation
4. Far outpace inflation

Question #4: What type of investment experience do you possess?
1. CDs, savings accounts, bonds, or bond funds
2. Stocks or stock funds, options or futures, managed accounts, international
3. Combination of the above types

Question #5: If you are looking for your investments to grow, approximately what rate of return would you want/need to meet your goals?
1. Less than five percent
2. Five to ten percent
3. Greater than ten percent

Question #6: How would you react if the value of your long-term investments declined by 10 percent in one year?

1. There may be market fluctuations, but I would be genuinely concerned if my investments value declined by ten percent.
2. I accept some market fluctuations, but I would be somewhat concerned if the investment's value declined by ten percent and remained there for more than a short period of time.
3. I generally invest for the long-term and would not be concerned.

Question #7: Which of the following best describes your reaction if the value of your portfolio declined 20 percent and remained there for more than a brief period of time?
1. I would be very concerned because I cannot accept fluctuations in the value of my portfolio.
2. I accept some market fluctuations, but I would be somewhat concerned if the value of my investments declined twenty percent.
3. I invest for long-term growth and would accept a twenty percent decline.

Question #8: What period of time will you use to measure the success of your investment portfolio?
1. Less than one year
2. Two to three years
3. Three to five years

Question #9: Which of the following best describes your feelings toward choosing your investments?

1. I would select investments with a low degree of risk.
2. I prefer to diversify with a mix of investments with the majority in low-risk categories.
3. I prefer to diversify with a balanced mix of risk categories.
4. I want the greatest possible returns, regardless of risk.

How to Get Your Risk Tolerance Score: Write the number of each answer in the boxes provided and total them here.

Total Score:

Based on your total score, your risk tolerance is:

9–12 = Low Risk Tolerance

13–16 = Low to Moderate Risk Tolerance

17–21 = Moderate Risk Tolerance

22–25 = Moderate to High Risk Tolerance

26–30 = Aggressive Risk Tolerance

Once we have your total score, we can determine how close your current investment portfolio matches your actual risk tolerance. If it doesn't, we can suggest ways to align your portfolio with your tolerance level. While most folks believe their investments already match their risk tolerance, we find the opposite is often true. With many clients, when they first enter our office, we find the risk level of their current portfolio far exceeds their risk tolerance. Let's look at this more closely with our longtime client, Jill.

When we first met Jill, she was sixty, recently divorced, and trying to make sure her money was hard at work. She had multiple investment accounts, all of which were 100 percent invested in the stock market. Jill told her previous advisor she didn't want big swings in her account, but she felt as if something was off. Once we got her score, we found her risk tolerance was firmly in the moderate range, but her current portfolio was designed to be incredibly aggressive. While this may have set her up for the possibility of some short-term gains, it dramatically increased her risk exposure—something she did not want.

We usually see these fears pop up as clients get closer to retirement. As the date grows near, more people seem to prefer avoiding big losses in their portfolios. We believe in having money in the market, but we also believe in using safer instruments with less volatility. This way you may avoid those big swings and hefty drops that send a soon-to-be retiree reeling.

What about Protecting Assets from Taxes?

We've covered the essential aspects of asset protection and investment planning, so let's shift our focus to another critical part of financial management: lowering your income tax bill. Optimizing your tax efficiency can help you minimize your tax burden and maximize the growth and preservation of your assets. In our next chapter, we'll examine the *three* tax categories, discuss strategies to help you reduce your tax burden, and look at a few case studies.

5

How to Structure Your Assets to Minimize Income Taxes

Let's talk about something so many people miss the mark on: *the actual position of their hard-earned money*. There are only three types of money, and I mean just three. Sure, hundreds of investments are out there, but no matter what you choose, your money will fall into one of these three critical categories: **taxable (nonqualified)**, **tax-deferred (qualified)**, or **tax-free**.

So what is the difference between a nonqualified and a qualified account? A qualified account (pre-taxed dollars) has been given the governmental stamp of approval, offering long-term tax deferral if you deposit your money into it. It's labeled as "qualified" due to the specific limitations and amounts you're permitted to deposit into these accounts. For example, a qualified IRA caps your yearly pretax contributions at $6,000 in 2023 (or $7,000 for those age fifty and older).

Nonqualified accounts (after-tax dollars), on the other hand, do not have the same tax advantages. But a nonqualified account, like a regular savings or brokerage account, doesn't limit the amount of after-tax money you can deposit. Therefore, the term "nonqualified" refers to the lack of government-imposed contribution limits for these accounts and their absence of the specific tax advantages qualified accounts offer.

Let's take a closer look at each of these three categories, starting with taxable accounts.

Taxable Accounts (Nonqualified)

The taxable category includes accounts where any growth or investment returns are taxed every year. There are a large number of accounts falling under this nonqualified umbrella. These include stocks, bonds, cash, savings accounts, certifications of deposits (CDs), and money market accounts. You may have noticed all of these accounts are taxable. This means each year, savings accounts, CDs, and money market accounts are going to churn out some interest, ideally adding to your existing pool of cash. But alas, Uncle Sam wants his cut, so you're obligated to pay taxes on those gains each year. A subtle difference in this category is individual stocks. An individual stock, if held for one year and then sold, will generate capital gains tax instead of ordinary income tax.

Suppose you put a dollar in a CD, money market account, or certain individual stocks and bonds. If the investment earns five cents in growth, that five cents is taxed at ordinary income rates. Every year, you'll be faced with the task of reporting and paying taxes on the growth they've generated. Even dividends from stocks fall into this taxable bucket. So, you must be prepared to part ways with a portion of those earnings, often at ordinary income rates, which can chip away at your overall returns.

Tax-Deferred Accounts (Qualified)

Our second category encompasses tax-deferred or tax-postponed accounts. Here's where the game changes a bit in your favor. When you contribute your money to retirement accounts such as traditional IRAs, 401(k)s, 403(b)s, or similar plans, you get to take a break from paying taxes on this money this year. Small business owners can also use some lesser-known savings vehicles like SIMPLE IRA and SEP-IRA to defer taxes. That's the beauty of it—postponing those taxes until later. It's like getting a temporary reprieve from your tax burden, allowing your dollars to grow and compound, which can significantly boost your nest egg over time. However, when you finally start withdrawing funds from these retirement accounts, you'll be on the hook for income taxes. So, while it's a strategic move to defer taxes during your high-earning years, planning for the eventual tax bill coming due during your retirement years is essential. In the next section, we will show you a strategy we use with our clients to mitigate some of those taxes.

Tax-Free Accounts

Here's the financial sweet spot: the tax-free category. This is where you've made the savvy choice to pay your taxes up front. By investing in accounts such as Roth IRAs, Roth 401(k)s, or even certain types of permanent life insurance, you've already handed over the tax dollars. But guess what? Once you've paid the price, all future growth and distributions from these accounts are entirely tax-free. Imagine that you've planted your money in a garden where the harvest is all yours, without Uncle Sam's hand reaching in to grab a share. It's a powerful way to maximize your retirement funds and protect yourself from potential future tax hikes. And let me tell you, it feels like a financial victory knowing your money is sheltered from the clutches of the tax collector. You can enjoy the fruits of your labor without the burden of income taxes down the road or the fear those taxes could increase in the future.

Most of the clients we see, come in with an unbalanced percentage in each of these categories. A mix we see frequently seems to be around 20 percent taxable, 70 percent tax-deferred, and 10 percent income-tax-free.

You may be fine with the status quo. But for many, a healthier balance such as 20 percent taxable, 40 percent tax-deferred, and 40 percent income-tax-free may allow them to manage their income and taxes more efficiently.

So why would I describe the initial percentage mix as suboptimal? Well, the problem lies in those tax-deferred accounts, which really should be labeled *"tax-postponed"* accounts. While it is advantageous to receive a current year reduction in your taxes, these accounts are actually just delaying the inevitable. Eventually, when you start drawing income out of those accounts, you'll have to face the music and pay the taxes. The idea used to be you would retire in a lower tax bracket than when you were working, but times are changing. Our country's national debt is ballooning. In September of 2018, the debt topped $22 trillion; near the end of 2023, that number is now well over $33 trillion.[10] By the time you read this book, we may be facing over a $40 trillion debt. We've got to face the facts. One day, this debt may cause tax hikes

---

10 "What is the National Debt?", https://fiscaldata.treasury.gov/americas-finance-guide/national-debt/. Accessed November 10, 2023.

affecting retirement, potentially undermining the whole tax-deferral strategy. This is why we're all about proactive planning and finding ways to manage taxes wisely, even before required minimum distributions (RMDs) kick in.

A question I often get is, "What should I do with the money in these accounts?" One strategic instrument we use for these tax-deferred or tax-postponed accounts is a Roth conversion. Roth conversions can carry money from tax-deferred accounts into tax-free territory. To reiterate, qualified money refers to funds in accounts already receiving a contribution-related tax deduction, including traditional IRAs, 401(k)s, or 403(b)s.

Of course, when you put the conversion in motion, you'll need to pay income taxes on the amount converted in the year of the conversion. Then, any further gains and distributions aren't subject to future taxes. Now you may be asking, "What about the tax code changes in 2026?" Well, fear not; according to current laws, Roth conversions are immune to those alterations. Currently, these accounts have no RMD. (There have been murmurs, however, suggesting the introduction of an RMD on Roths, even though the distributions remain nontaxable, but thankfully it has yet to happen.)

While looking to the future is good, let's return to the current state of affairs. When you invest in a Roth, either through contribution or conversion, you pay the taxes up front. From then on, any future distribution is tax-free. Plus, there's no time limit; you can let your money marinate in the Roth for as long as you fancy. And the icing on the cake is that you can transfer it to your heirs. Again, there have been discussions about changing this rule, but there's nothing on the books as of this writing.

Tax Planning Strategies and the Current Tax Code

While there are numerous sophisticated tax planning strategies involving trusts we collaborate on with accountants and tax attorneys, we won't delve into those complexities in this book. Instead, let's focus on a simple yet effective strategy we can apply right now and utilize actively until 2025.

Here's the rationale behind our proactive approach and what it has to do with the tax code. The current tax code is set to expire in January of 2026; at that time, it is scheduled to revert back to the 2017 tax code. The current code is based on the Tax Cuts and Jobs Act (TCJA), which was passed during the Trump administration. The TCJA was no ordinary tax cut. This legislation was one of the most significant overhauls of the tax code in decades, making substantial changes to both individual and corporate tax law. The intention was to boost the economy by slashing corporate tax rates and providing temporary tax relief to individuals.

Before the Trump tax cuts, the corporate tax rate sat at a hefty 35 percent. Afterward, that number was whittled down to a flat 21 percent. This was a game-changer for

American businesses. For individuals and families, the changes were more nuanced. Tax brackets were tweaked, and tax rates were generally lowered. For example, if you were in the 15 percent tax bracket before, you found yourself in the much more palatable 12 percent bracket post-TCJA. Similarly, those in the 25 percent bracket were bumped down to 22 percent.

However, it's important to remember these cuts were designed with a sunset clause, meaning they expire after 2025. Once this tax code expires, most individuals are likely to experience an increase in income taxes, typically ranging from 3 percent to 7 percent. So, how can we be proactive and defend against this impending scenario?

We would want to utilize the current tax brackets to our advantage, aiming to withdraw money from your qualified plans while keeping it in a lower bracket. You might wonder, how can we achieve that? Well, it's all about understanding the progressive nature of tax brackets.

The first tax bracket is zero percent, meaning a portion of your income is not taxed at all. The subsequent brackets have higher tax rates, such as 10 percent and 12 percent. So, for example, using our strategy, we could take $20,000 from IRAs and $52,000 from Social Security and still manage to stay within the zero percent tax bracket. Using that example, it's also possible to withdraw additional funds from IRAs while still remaining in the 12 percent bracket.

Mark & Brenda:
Applied Early for Social Security

Section 1	Enter Here ↓	Page 2, 1040		Original
Wages, Salaries, Tips		1	→	0
Tax-Exempt Interest		2a	0	
Interest Income		2b	→	0
Qualified Dividends		3a	0	
Ordinary Dividends		3b	→	0
Gross IRA Distributions		4a	54,617	
Taxable IRAs		4b	→	54,617
Gross Pensions		5a	0	
Taxable Pensions		5b	→	0
Gross Social Security		6a	24,000	24,000
Taxable S.S.		6b	85%	20,400

Section 2	Breakdown of Taxes			
Tax Year	2023	2023		
Taxes	Original	Revised	Rev $ Diff	% Changed
Pg 2, Ln 16	4,878	5,120	0	0%
AMT, Sch 2,L1	0	0	0	
NIT, Sch 2,L8	0	0	0	
Federal	4,878	5,120	0	0%
State	1,739	1,752	0	5.3%
Taxes	Original	Revised	Rev $ Diff	% Changed
Total Tax	**6,617**	**6,617**	**0**	**0%**

Mark & Brenda: Applied Early for Social Security

Section 3	
$24,000	Social Security
$54,617	IRA
$78,617	Total
$75,017	Taxable
$30,700	Std. Ded.
$44,317	Taxable
12%	(Top Tax Bracket)
$4,878	Federal Tax
$1,739	NC State Tax
$6,617	Total Tax
After-Tax Income	
$72,000/year	
$6,000/month	

By carefully managing your withdrawals, we can help ensure the money from your IRAs, combined with your existing income, stays within the 12 percent bracket. This way, you minimize the tax impact and optimize your retirement income. We previously showed you this in chapter 2. But let's look back at our example couples, Mark and Brenda and John and Connie. The graphs below illustrate these numbers, as well as the way applying for Social Security income early can affect your ability to StayRetired™.

Remember Mark and Brenda? While they are both over sixty-five, they rushed into Social Security before

John & Connie: Used Strategy to Apply for Social Security

Section 1	Enter Here ↓	Page 1, 1040		Original
Wages, Salaries, Tips		1	→	
Tax-Exempt Interest		2a	0	
Interest Income		2b	→	
Qualified Dividends		3a	0	
Ordinary Dividends		3b	→	
Gross IRA Distributions		4a	20,000	
Taxable IRAs		4b	→	20,000
Gross Pensions		5a	0	
Taxable Pensions		5b	→	
Gross Social Security		6a	52,000	52,000
Taxable S.S.		6b	15%	7,700

Section 2	Breakdown of Taxes			
Tax Year	2023	2023		
Taxes	Original	Revised	Rev $ Diff	% Changed
Pg 2, Ln 16	0	0	0	0%
AMT, Sch 2,L1	0	0	0	
NIT, Sch 2,L8	0	0	0	
Federal	0	0	0	0%
State	0	0	0	5.3%
Taxes	Original	Revised	Rev $ Diff	% Changed
Total Tax	0	0	0	0%

John & Connie:
Used Strategy to Apply for Social Security

Section 3	
$20,000	Social Security
$52,000	IRA
$72,000	Total
$27,700	Taxable
$29,121	Std. Ded.
$-1,421	Taxable
0%	Tax Bracket
After-Tax Income	
$72,000/year	
$6,000/month	

their benefits could fully mature, collecting $24,000. But, to meet their income goal, they've got to pull a whopping $54,872 from their IRA. With the tax codes we're dealing with, they'll be shelling out $6,872 to the taxman. Now you may be thinking "Well, that isn't too bad!" And sure, it leaves them with $72,000 of after-tax income, with 85 percent of their Social Security benefits getting taxed. It may sound fair, but what if I told you there's a way to avoid leaving all that money on the table?

Let's look at our other example couple, John and Connie. With our strategic guidance, they chose to delay their Social Security benefits until the timing was just right, and now they are in a much better position with $52,000 a year in benefits. This means they only need $20,000 more to meet the requirements of their spending plan. But here's the kicker: Not a single cent of that $20,000 is taxable. And their after-tax income is $72,000, the same as before, but without giving the taxman a cut.

Even if they needed to take it up a notch to $92,000 a year, for example, we could adjust. By taking a distribution from a Roth IRA, they could have $92,000 with no income tax. All told, John and Connie would have almost $7,000 more in their pockets at the end of the year. All it takes is a bit of savvy planning and tax code knowledge.

It's crucial we strategically bring money out of your IRAs while keeping you in a low tax bracket. This approach empowers us to proactively manage your taxes throughout your retirement journey, making it a potentially effective tax control technique. All of this highlights the importance of strategic planning, especially as it relates to positioning and withdrawal.

Positioning and Withdrawal

Here's the reason behind our approach: Once you reach the age of seventy-three, you'll be required to start taking mandatory distributions from your qualified plans, called RMD (required minimum distribution). Unfortunately, you won't have a choice in the matter. This is why we advocate for a proactive strategy, rather than a passive one. This strategy would allow you to move some of your funds out of your qualified plans before the government mandates it.

By executing this proactive plan, we position ourselves to potentially pay less income tax than we would in the future. It's all about strategic timing and optimizing withdrawals to minimize tax liability. With careful planning and implementation, we can take advantage of the current tax landscape and help maintain control over your taxes, especially while the current tax code is still in place. By taking advantage of the existing brackets and having a well-thought-out strategy, we can navigate potential tax increases and work toward keeping your tax burden as low as possible throughout retirement.

Now That We've Put You to Sleep, Let's Talk about Something Fun

While the conversation around taxes may not be the most exciting part of retirement, it's a piece of the puzzle we can't ignore. It's all about keeping more of your hard-earned money in your pocket so you have the freedom to do the things you love. But rest assured; this isn't all retirement is about. It's time to put the calculators away for a moment and start envisioning the life you want to lead once work is off the table. Let's turn our focus to all the fun awaiting you in retirement. In the next chapter, we will explore how to plan and save for all the post-retirement fun you've been working so hard for all these years.

Joe and Debbie - Niagra Falls

6
How to Plan and Save for Post-Retirement Fun

While I want to jump right into the fun part, let me start by telling a story illustrating why it's so important to live your life to the fullest while you can.

In 2012, the health of my in-laws began to decline. My father-in-law faced a life-threatening situation in 2013 due to a failing heart valve replaced a decade earlier. Despite the longevity mechanical valves can often have, he chose a bioprosthetic pig valve because it was quieter and, honestly, he didn't think he would outlive it. When the bioprosthetic started to fail, my wife, Debbie, fought to get him into a clinical trial for a new procedure, a pioneering operation that has been done hundreds of times across the country since. However, while his health was still shaky, my mother-in-law was then diagnosed with cancer. Debbie spent forty weekends in 2017 driving from our home in Charlotte, North Carolina, to her parents' home in Supply, North Carolina—a three-and-a-half-hour trip one way—to help care for them. Overall, it took an incredible toll on both of us.

During this stressful time, I came to the realization Debbie and I hadn't had a proper getaway in years. So in 2018, we decided we were well overdue for a vacation, and we set our sights on Niagara Falls. A few friends advised us to visit the Canadian side; we hadn't been to Canada in quite some time, so we were excited. Debbie and I were not only looking forward to the gorgeous view of the falls, but also for the newer boats situated on the Canadian side. The boats on the American side are upward of fifty years old, while the ones on the Canadian side were only five years old. Not only that, but then we found out the American boats didn't have bathrooms! We knew we had made the right call in heading to the Canadian side of the falls.

So we took a train ride from Albany, New York, up to Niagara Falls, stopping at the Canadian border. The train had to go through customs, so everyone had to depart the train and then get back on (a bit of pain). After the border check, we finally made it to Canada and Niagara Falls. The picture you see (on page 92) is us at the Falls, and yes, the boats had bathrooms.

Here's the point of the story: Spend your money while you're alive and able to enjoy it. We put recreation on the back burner while we dealt with work, family emergencies, and everything else under the sun. But this isn't all there is to life. You need to go places and do the things you've always wanted to do while you're healthy. Trust me, most vacation spots involve a lot of walking, so take advantage of your good health. Getting on and off the train and walking around the boat to see the beautiful sights would have been impossible if Debbie and I hadn't been in good shape. And if you work yourself to death and save all your money, what really happens to it? *The sad reality is the average time it takes to spend an inheritance is just eighteen months.* So, instead of only worrying about what you are leaving behind, focus on having fun while you are still here.

The Importance of Having Fun and Staying Active during Retirement

I've said this before, but I really can't stress this enough: **It's your money, and you've earned the right to spend it.** You may be asking, "Okay, where?" Well, a good place to start is with the remaining items on your bucket list. What haven't you done that you would love to try? You can start your bucket list with the top ten places you want to visit and the top ten things you want to do. These may overlap, but it will give you a good idea of what planning direction to head in.

Once you've got your list, you'll want to figure out the cost. Some bucket list items might even be free. If volunteering at your local mission is on your list, it's completely free. On the other hand, if setting off on a tour of Europe for a month is more your style, it's going to take some budgeting. We advise people to pick one large activity (something taking between a week and a month) and one small activity (something taking up to four days) each year. Once you've chosen your activities, all you need to do is research the costs and start planning.

Also, there's no reason to wait until retirement to start ticking items off your bucket list. Most people have several weeks of vacation time each year while working, so make sure to use all of the time when you can. A lot of folks end up with PTO days they never end up cashing out—and you can't take PTO with you. Plan a trip while you're still working and get a taste of what retirement could be like. Use vacation time to prepare, enjoy, and decompress. Why? Because, again, you want to take these adventures while you're as healthy as possible. The reality of most vacations is you are going to end up traversing cities, going up flights of stairs, and racking up multiple miles each day. So, start planning, start moving, and start living your dreams while you can.

Once you have the expenses of your trip sorted, you'll want to think about the particulars of your life back at home. You don't want to be worrying about anything while you are on vacation, so it's important to ensure everything continues to run smoothly while you are gone. Ask yourself the following questions:

- Who will pick up your mail while you're gone?
- Do you have any subscriptions you need to pause or put on hold?
- Who is keeping an eye on your house?
- Who is going to take care of your pets? Are you boarding them or having someone drop by daily?
- Do you need to stop your newspaper subscriptions and mail delivery?

These small details need to be factored into your planning. Make sure you've considered everything, so you don't return from a fantastic trip to a disaster at home. Nobody wants to come home to a flooded house while they've been off enjoying their holiday. If you're proactive and plan well, you can ensure you have a worry-free trip and an intact and undamaged home to return to.

Another factor to consider is self-planning versus hiring a travel agent. Let's use a personal example here. Debbie and I were recently planning a trip to Washington, DC, to visit the Smithsonian for a couple of days. We were doing all the planning, and I have to admit, it was a bit confusing. When I was a kid, my aunt who lived in DC used to be our guide. She would tell us the opening hours, the best places to park, the must-see exhibits, etc. She was basically a professional DC guide, but now without her guidance, we had to try and figure things out on our own.

I don't live there, and I don't plan trips every day. It took us quite a bit of time to figure out which exhibits we wanted to see during our short visit. The level of assistance you'll need really depends on how much time you have to plan and the complexity of the trip. If I had to do it again, I would get the help of a professional so I wouldn't waste any time or money. Funny enough, this exact same thought could be applied to financial planning. Why feel your way around in the dark, burning up time and your hard-earned cash, when you could just seek out the help of a professional?

Retirement as a Lifestyle: Leisure Versus Travel

Speaking of planning, let's talk about the big picture stuff. Instead of just looking at a single trip, consider how you will live your life in retirement as a whole. One question I ask my clients is, "What does retirement mean to you?" The answer varies from person to person.

Some folks prefer the comfort of their home. I have a pair of clients who own cute, dog-sized mini-horses on a ten-acre plot. They're more than content to stay at home with their horses, land, and big barn. They don't feel the slightest need to hit the beach, hop in an RV, or fly abroad. These people were more than happy to stay at home and receive deliveries during the pandemic. They are probably two of Amazon's favorite customers! But let me tell you, they're in the minority. Most people yearn for a bit of adventure and travel when they hang up their work boots.

My advice always starts with figuring out what you want to do in retirement, determining how much it's going to cost, and deciding whether you can afford it. Maybe you are a couple who prefer to take one big trip a year and visit the out-of-state grandkids a few times. You should calculate the travel costs associated with your visits and big trips and factor them into your income plan. You should also consider the external events that may affect your travel. These aren't always negative; sometimes, due to events such as COVID, these trips can cost less than expected because travel companies need customers.

Every Trip Doesn't Have to Be Extravagant or Expensive, but Watch Out for Those Hidden Costs

At the end of the day, while staying home may be cheaper, it doesn't mean you can't plan for travel. Even if you take one big trip a year, it doesn't mean you need to spend a hefty sum of money. It's all about looking at your income plan and determining what you can reasonably afford. A short trip can fit neatly into a budget, while longer trips will naturally increase costs. In addition to length, you also have to consider what equipment you'll need to complete the trip, like an RV.

For instance, two of our clients, Thomas and Martha, rented an RV for two months, touring twenty-five different states. They kept their home while experiencing the grandeur of places like the Great Salt Lake and the Black Hills. This meant they needed to account for the costs they would be incurring as property owners, along with the costs of RV rental, gas prices, food costs, and everything else they needed for their trip. You'll also have to keep in mind that some of your expenses could fluctuate based on economic conditions. It's important to take external variables into account.

If You Decide to Move, Consider Every Component of the Situation

If you decide you are happier at home but aren't sure where your home will be, there are a few factors to consider, including climate. I have clients who moved from Ohio to Florida because they preferred the warmer winters. While they love the sun, they weren't thinking about all the other consequences of the move. Now those clients have had to deal with increased property taxes, a new mortgage, and other rising costs.

If you want to think about getting a second home in another state, you'll need to budget for it. You'll also have to think about things such as taxes. For example, states like Florida and Tennessee have no income tax, but they do have higher sales tax. If you have properties in two different states, you might not get full tax benefits. In such cases, we can help you evaluate the best options based on your circumstances.

Remember, retirement isn't a one-size-fits-all situation. Some may want to get out on the road or focus on home improvement and building their castle, while others will want to pour money into their hobbies. Planning and financial consultation can help make the transition from preretirement to postretirement much smoother, leaving you to enjoy the lifestyle you've worked hard to earn. Part of this won't be possible without overcoming the guilt of spending.

Overcoming the Guilt of Spending

First off, let's be clear: No matter how much wealth one has, from $100,000 to $5 million, the fear of running out of money is universal. It's one of the biggest fears every retiree has, and it's quite understandable. You've worked hard to build up your money, so it can feel difficult to use any of it.

As an advisor, one of the most rewarding parts of my job is to encourage people to enjoy the fruits of their labor. Let me tell you about a couple I know, Jacob and Emily. Emily is in her late seventies, while Jacob just turned eighty. Pre-COVID, they would take two to four domestic trips a year, enjoying various spots around the United States. Then COVID struck, health problems cropped up, and their adventurous spirit faded. Suddenly, getting them to spend their own money became a challenge.

So, I did what I do with all my clients: *reassure them it is okay to spend.* I told them it was okay to splurge on a dream trip or get the $30,000 truck Jacob had been looking at. Why? Because if you don't spend it, you may lose it. Research shows 70 percent of wealthy families lose their wealth by the second generation and a staggering 90 percent by the third.[11]

I've personally experienced just how quickly an inheritance can disappear. When my grandmother passed away, she left an estate of about $100,000. My portion was around $8,000. Within three days, the money was gone, eaten up by bills and needs. And trust me, this disappearing act can happen with much larger amounts too.

From Enjoying Wealth to Planning for Health

While it's important to embrace the joy and freedom that comes with spending wisely in retirement, it's also essential to prepare for unforeseen circumstances that might arise. It's all part of a well-rounded retirement plan; as we age, health can become a significant factor in our financial planning. Therefore, it's crucial to spend some time considering long-term healthcare choices.

In the next chapter, we'll dive into how to prepare for and navigate the complex world of long-term healthcare. Stay with me, folks, as we journey into this important aspect of retirement planning.

---

11 I. Pino. (2023). "Generational Wealth Explained: What It is and How Experts Say You Can Work to Build and Protect It." *Fortune Recommends.* https://fortune.com/recommends/investing/generational-wealth-explained/

7

Reviewing Long-Term Healthcare Choices

Research by the Department of Health and Human Services shows that 70 percent of adults who survive to age sixty-five develop the need for long-term support before they die, while 48 percent receive some paid care over their lifetime.[12] As we age, the likelihood of needing some form of long-term care assistance grows significantly. There are a number of choices to be made, misconceptions, and vital considerations related to long-term healthcare. The first step to protecting your assets and getting the care you need is to understand this process fully.

---

12 Office of the Assistant Secretary for Planning and Education (2019, April 3). "What Is the Lifetime Risk of Needing and Receiving Long-Term Services and Supports?," https://aspe.hhs.gov/reports/what-lifetime-risk-needing-receiving-long-term-services-supports.

Long-Term Care: A Growing Need

People are getting older:

- Seniors (65+) make up 14% of the US population
- Seniors will make up 20% of the US population within the next 20 years.

10,000+ people are turning 65 every day.

People are living longer:

- People are living longer than ever and "dramatic" gains in life expectancy show no sign of slowing down. (WHO 5/13/13)

Understanding Long-Term Care

I hear it constantly, and the point can't be overstated: We are facing a healthcare crisis. Whether it's needing someone to care for a loved one at home, in an assisted living facility, or in a nursing home, nearly everyone is worried about losing all of their money to access these services. I've heard my clients say, "I don't want to give all my money, all my assets, and the rest of my life to a nursing home. I worked too hard to accumulate this wealth. If I can't spend it enjoying my retirement, I want it to go to my children and other loved ones." This is a perfectly valid way to feel, and it's indicative of a significant shift in focus I see at this point in many people's lives. It's not fun to think about, but as time goes on, the concerns generally shift from vacations and luxuries to the reality of illness and the need for care. So, what qualifies you for long-term care?

In most cases, any chronic or disabling condition means you can qualify for long-term care. The severity of these conditions can often be determined by looking at certain "activities of daily living." Referred to as ADLs, these activities are ones most people tend to perform every day without assistance. Now, the inability to do two or more of these activities may mean you qualify to receive long-term care. Let's take a look at each of these six activities a bit more closely.

Activities of Daily Living

1. **Transferring:** This ADL refers to the ability to move around on your own, including getting out of bed, standing up from a seated position in a chair or couch, or traveling from one room to another. Think of transferring as anything relating to mobility and the capability to navigate your environment safely. Without the ability to move in a safe manner, a person can become bedridden or restricted in movement, limiting independence and overall quality of life. You likely test your transference abilities every day when you wake up. Think about it: You open your eyes, throw off your blanket, put your feet on the ground, and get up.

If you can do this, you've proven your transferring capabilities.

2. **Continence:** This one is a bit delicate, but without mincing words, this ADL is about your ability to control your bladder and bowel functions. It means knowing when to use the bathroom or managing incontinence products, if needed. This is essential for personal hygiene and comfort. Losing control over this aspect of life could lead to some very embarrassing moments, not to mention health issues, if the problem isn't managed correctly. When I get up in the morning and walk to the bathroom, I'm not only transferring but also checking that my continence is okay. Basically, if I don't wet myself, then I know I'm still in control! Thank goodness, I still am.

3. **Bathing:** While continence is essential for hygiene, it isn't quite as important as the ability to bathe oneself. This ADL also includes managing personal grooming, such as shaving or brushing teeth and maintaining proper hair care. Losing your ability to bathe isn't just about being presentable in social situations; cleanliness can also contribute to emotional well-being. Feeling clean and well-groomed boosts self-esteem, overall mood, and motivation. Here's how I think of it: If you can get yourself into the shower or tub and wash yourself, you are doing fine in this category.

4. **Dressing:** This category refers to one's ability to pick out and put on the proper attire for different situations. To satisfy the requirements of this ADL, you'll need to understand what clothes make sense for different weather, in addition to remembering how to button shirts, zip zippers, and tie your shoes. Putting on clothes isn't only important for showing off your sense of fashion, it also shows you are aware of your surroundings and environment. Being able to clothe yourself contributes to personal dignity and a sense of identity.

5. **Toileting:** This ADL can sometimes be confused with continence, but the two are distinct. While continence means you can manage your bodily functions, toileting concerns your ability to use the facilities on your own, including cleaning yourself up afterward. Using the toilet independently is a crucial aspect of personal privacy. In addition, toileting takes a sense of coordination to help prevent slips and falls. If you can get on and off the toilet (and clean up after), then you don't have to worry about this category.

6. **Eating:** The last ADL isn't about whipping up a gourmet meal or lighting up the grill for an outdoor barbeque. The eating ADL is more about the simple act of getting food from a plate

to your mouth. Some activities in this category include using utensils, cutting food into pieces you can manage, chewing and swallowing without difficulty, and drinking from a cup or straw. Eating isn't just about getting yourself nourished but also about social engagement. Humans have been connecting over meals for thousands of years, and being able to eat independently allows you to participate in these social activities.

For those who do not qualify for long-term care, a regular day might start this way: You wake up in the morning, slide out of bed, walk to the bathroom, use the bathroom, bathe, dress yourself, and eat breakfast. This small morning routine covers all six ADLs in short order. On the other hand, if you can't perform two of these without assistance, or you are suffering from cognitive impairments such as Alzheimer's or dementia, you likely qualify to receive long-term care.

Understanding Real Costs: Debunking Misconceptions and Exploring Who Pays for Long-Term Care

When planning for long-term care, it's easy to get lost in a maze of costs, misconceptions, and decision-making for who pays what. The financial aspect of long-term care is often perceived as a simple equation of dollars and cents, but the reality is far more complex. It's not just about nursing homes or draining personal savings;

the landscape includes various care settings, insurance policies, government programs, and personal choices.

One common misconception most people associate with long-term care is that it always takes place in a nursing home. But the reality is only about 20 percent of actual care provided is in a long-term care facility. Believe it or not, more than 80 percent is at home or in a rehabilitation facility.

As far as who pays for long-term care, there are usually two primary sources footing the bill:

- **Public Side:** Medicare, Veterans Administration aid plan, and long-term Medicaid
- **Private Side:** Personal assets and long-term care insurance policy

On the public side, the two programs most people have heard of are Medicare and Medicaid. So, what is the difference between these programs when it comes to long-term care? Comparing the two programs is like comparing apples and oranges. There are some similarities, but way more differences. Let's explore some common misinterpretations about these two programs.

Medicare

A lot of people believe Medicare will cover an extended long-term care event. But here's the truth: Medicare pays for doctors and hospitals for those *over sixty-five years old*. It will cover some long-term care expenses, but generally covers only short-term skilled care. But, and this is crucial, if Medicare is going to pay for a "long-term care expense," it's because you're getting better. Don't get confused by stories like Aunt Sally's "completely free" hip surgery; if she isn't recovering, Medicare stops paying.

Medicaid

Medicaid is the number one payer of long-term care expenses. But be aware, there are strict income and asset limits, even though some assets may be exempt. Income limits can range from $1,500 to $3,000 a month; the asset limit in most states is $2,000. Don't worry; there are ways to navigate this. Medicaid allows asset protection for a well spouse (or "community spouse"). For a person to qualify for these classifications, they must be the spouse of an individual who is receiving Medicaid-funded long-term care in a nursing home or through a Home and Community-based Services [HCBS] Medicaid Waiver. It's also important to note that there are opportunities to protect more than $2,000.

Whether you use your assets, long-term care insurance, Medicare, Medicaid, or anything else, having a long-term care plan is often worth the money. Why is this? Well, I usually narrow it down to two main reasons:

1. *It allows you to set money aside.* This isn't just a financial safety net; it's a way to ensure your family

can provide the care you need without unnecessary additional financial strain.
2. *It protects your assets.* A well-structured long-term care plan safeguards what you've worked so hard to build.

Private Pay: Your First Line of Defense

Before the government steps in to lend a hand, they want you to take the lead. Whether it's a state plan or a federal plan such as Medicaid, you're in the driver's seat. Now, for those of you who are thinking about self-insuring, here's something eye-opening. According to the big players, like Genworth,[13] who have done plenty of research in long-term care, you need to have between $5 and $6 million dollars in assets to be fully self-insured. So, if you've got more, you might be on easy street. But, if you're below this threshold, experts say you should sit up and take notice.

Understanding Where Care Happens and the Different Types of Care

When we tackle long-term care, the first question to be answered is where you want to receive care when you are sick. The answer can dramatically change how much you end up paying. For instance, if you're in Pennsylvania, the

---

13 Genworth. (2022, June 2). "Cost of Care Report." https://www.genworth.com/aging-and-you/finances/cost-of-care.html/

cost may be in the neighborhood of $16,000 in a nursing home, while in North Carolina, you could be looking at between $8,000 to $10,000 per month. These costs all depend on the location and level of care.

Long-Term Care: A Growing Need

If **Assistant Living** care is needed:

- 1.8 years (avg time) x $52,800 Annual Cost = **$95,040**

If **Nursing Home** care is needed:

- 2.5 years (avg time) x $93,096 Annual Cost = **$232,740**

Total Facility care:

- Avg. 4.3 Years = **$327,780***

If **In Home** care is needed:

- 4.3 years x $219,000 Annual Cost = **$941,700***

*Average in Charlotte, NC

* *The figures in this chart are from Genworth's Cost of Care in 2021, which is the latest year these figures were compiled at the time of this publication.*

You'll need to think about the different types of care. While most folks want to be cared for at home, that's often the most expensive option. The average time someone spends in a long-term care facility, for example, a nursing home, is 4.3 years. This is just an average, as this varies, and the need for care can increase with certain illnesses or degenerative discascs. If we are looking at the averages in my home city of Charlotte, North Carolina, twenty-four-hour care at home could cost you around $941,000 for 4.3 years. If you want to pay that price for comfort, that's perfectly fine. The costs could be significantly lower if time was split between an assisted living facility and a nursing home. On average, folks spend 1.8 years in an assisted living facility at an annual cost of $52,000 (so a total of $95,040) and a nursing home for an average of 2.5 years at a price of $232,000. So, your total average facility care will be around $327,780.

Cost and Leverage Versus Liquidation

I won't sugarcoat it: This care is expensive. Whether you want to be at home or need specialized care, the numbers can add up quickly. But understanding your options and desires, not to mention planning ahead, can go a long way to preserving your quality of life. A big part of this planning is figuring out where this money is going to come from. We'll also have to answer the age-old question: liquidate or leverage?

If we are talking about liquidating assets to pay for your care, the first step is figuring out what asset will be liquidated. Is it going to be a stock account, your IRA, or maybe an old annuity? You could also use bonds, mutual funds, and your 401(k). In some cases, you may even have enough stashed away in checking and savings to cover the bill. Whatever the source may be, a common question to think at this point is, "Instead of burning up my assets, ***a.k.a. liquidating my assets***, is there a better way to pay for care?" The answer is yes, by *leveraging* those same assets.

Leveraging Your Assets: The Wise Approach

When it comes to leveraging assets and long-term care, there are really three different types of long-term care solutions we can explore: **traditional plans**, **life insurance-based plans**, and **hybrid long-term care plans**. We will also discuss the Pension Protection Act, an important piece of legislation giving you a way to create tax-advantaged funds to pay for your long-term care.

Traditional Plans

So, what do we know about long-term care insurance? Well, in effect, you're sharing the risk with an insurance company. For those who are healthy (or reasonably so), this can be a great boon to your assets. But there is one major obstacle: Acceptance of these plans is based almost entirely on your health. If you have certain preexisting conditions, you might not qualify.

As for the details of a traditional long-term care policy, that starts with talking about benefit amount. This is usually represented as the daily, monthly, and annual amounts, as well as the term of coverage. You can think of these amounts as a pool of money you can draw from. If you have a $6,000 a month plan, but you only need $2,000 in one particular month, the other $4,000 isn't thrown away; it's still there for future use.

Let's now talk about the payment period and how the waiver or premium works. Say you have a $200-a-day benefit ($6,000 a month) and a five-year plan. That's a $360,000 pool of money to work with. If we did an optional 3 percent simple inflation protection rider, the pool would grow to $467,000 in twenty years. This can help ensure your benefits keep up with the rising costs of care. Bear in mind most of these plans have a "ninety-day elimination period," which means you will be forced to pay from your assets for those ninety days once you are qualified. So, during this time, you'll have to figure out which asset the money comes from. An added benefit for many plans is a zero-elimination period for home healthcare. This gives you even more incentive to have at least a portion of the care administered in the comfort of your own home.

However, "traditional" long-term care plans we are describing seem to have become less popular. The primary reason is these are "if you don't use them, you lose them" plans. These long-term care benefits don't leave any money to you or your heirs if it isn't used up. Second, there is the real possibility of rate increases that come with these plans.

Life Insurance-Based Plans

The second option available is life insurance with a long-term care rider. Suppose you have $300,000 of death benefit coverage. If you were to use a monthly figure of $6,000 for your care needs, it would provide you with fifty months of care. The key point is this pool of money does not increase; it stays at $300,000. It's not going to increase over time. Some folks short-pay this coverage using a five-pay or ten-pay, meaning they'll pay the policy over five or ten years instead of over their lifetime. A five-pay or ten-pay can be a suitable option for those who wish to fully pay for the coverage in a shorter time frame.

In addition to benefits such as a waiver of premium, which waives premiums if you start using the benefits for care, you also get the benefit of flexibility. If you need long-term care, you can use the $300,000 as an accelerated benefit to pay for it. Each month the benefit is accessed, the death benefit decreases. If only a portion of the death benefit is used, the remaining death benefit will still go to your loved ones. If it's not used at all, the full death benefit goes to your heirs or spouse. You will have to deal with the ninety-day elimination period; however, for home healthcare, this can be zero days, meaning the coverage starts immediately.

Hybrid Long-Term Care Plans: The Unlimited Option

The third type, which has become very popular recently, is the hybrid plan. There are a few reasons why these types of plans are gaining traction. For one, some hybrid plans give you the ability to have unlimited coverage. Imagine having $300,000 at $6,000 a month, but it never runs out. Hybrid plans can provide an endless reservoir until a person's death. While there may be a monthly limit, the overall fund is unlimited. Another reason for their popularity is that they allow individuals the opportunity to take a lump sum from a nonperforming asset and use it to fund the entire policy at once. You can just put the money in and be done with it, which is a more proactive move for those who prefer to have things squared away.

Hybrid plans often have the same ninety-day elimination period as life insurance-based plans. While it is not as significant as what's offered in other plans, there are provisions allowing you to waive premiums. In addition, these plans provide a long-term care benefit for those who live longer and a death benefit for those who pass away. You can even quit the plan and get some or all of your money back. This trio of options provides unparalleled flexibility and ensures the money invested isn't locked away ineffectively. The label we use for these plans is **Live, Quit or Die**. If you **Live,** you access the long-term care benefit; if you **Quit,** you can get some or all of your money back; or if you **Die,** then your heirs get a death benefit. Bottom line with these plans, someone is going to receive a benefit for the money you have invested in the plan.

Hybrid plans are truly a blend of the best features, tailored to provide robust coverage and adaptability. Whether you're considering leveraging an existing asset or simply seeking a versatile plan catering to various potential needs, the hybrid long-term care plan offers an appealing option resonating with contemporary requirements and preferences.

Pension Protection Act

One vital piece of the puzzle that can really make long-term care planning more manageable concerns the Pension Protection Act annuity. In 2006, Congress did something pretty clever. They passed a law to open up a pathway for people to take money from their insurance or an existing annuity and use it to buy a long-term care policy. The provisions relating to long-term care and annuities came into effect in 2010, just a little while before the first of the baby boomers turned sixty-five. The best part? This exchange would be **income-tax-free**, and it would lead to income-tax-free long-term care benefits.

This wasn't just a law they passed on a whim. It was actually something done with foresight and an understanding of the real needs people would have as they approached retirement and possibly long-term care. You might be wondering how this plays out in the real world. Picture this: You have an underperforming annuity, something that's just not doing what you want it to. It's sitting there and has some gains, but it's not really shining. Thanks to this Pension Protection Act, you can take the basis (which are your contributions) and those gains, transfer them, and throw them right into a long-term care policy. And here's the kicker: All those gains just muddling along in the annuity become tax-free to you when used for long-term care. That's not just intelligent planning; that's turning a potential problem into a solution.

Medicaid Planning: What You May Not Know

We've covered what you need to know about long-term care, so it's time to take a closer look at a really misunderstood subject: *Medicaid planning.* In my thirty years in the financial services industry, I have never seen an area of planning so guarded by the gatekeepers. Medicaid has always been a planning subject nobody wanted to explain, but we intend to change that. In our next chapter, we'll look at what Medicaid planning does, why it is important, and what it means to the families who can access it.

8
Medicaid Planning
It's Not Just for Poor People

DISCLAIMER: *It's important to note that our team collaborates with a specialized group that expertly navigates these complicated Medicaid guidelines. They understand the intricacies of this type of planning and follow all applicable laws and rules in the states where they operate. This specialized group works with Certified Medicaid Planners™ as well as estate attorneys in all fifty states. Through strategic planning and making full use of existing rules, many individuals can qualify for Medicaid benefits while still keeping a good amount of their assets.*

Medicaid can serve as a viable option for certain aspects of long-term care planning. This should not take the place of a good long-term care plan but can act as a backstop if things do not go as planned. I think this is best demonstrated by the experience of our client Beth.

Last year, Beth received a devastating diagnosis of breast cancer. While this was tough, she was fortunate enough to live in North Carolina, which has a unique program for her situation. Because Beth had only her home in her name without any other significant assets, this program stated she qualified for Medicaid. The key factor in this was her husband's financial foresight. You see, her husband had previously inherited a substantial amount of money, which he wisely kept solely in his name. As a result, these funds didn't factor into Beth's assets, and she was able to qualify for Medicaid.

Tragically, her husband passed away just six months later—his death was sudden and unexpected. While their jointly titled home naturally transferred to Beth, his will stated all other assets should be bequeathed to her as well. If this significant sum of money had been directly transferred into Beth's checking or savings account, she would have lost her Medicaid eligibility instantly. *This is where prudent planning made all the difference.*

The strategy used was to funnel the funds into an asset protection trust during the probate process by having her disclaim the inheritance. Normally a disclaimer will be treated as a transfer of assets and penalized by Medicaid, but the program she was approved under did not have a transfer penalty. The beauty of this arrangement was that the money remained out of reach for Medicaid purposes. Beth retained her Medicaid coverage, ensuring that she could continue her crucial cancer treatments without any financial disruptions. In the end, her assets were successfully safeguarded.

With proactive Medicaid planning, even the most trying times can be easier to bear. However, there are a lot of misconceptions floating around about Medicaid, that can make it harder to utilize. One misconception is that Medicaid is strictly for poor people; in reality, Medicaid is a significant source of long-term care coverage in the US, even for those who have a significant amount of money. People also commonly confuse Medicaid with Medicare. While Medicare does cover some long-term care expenses, Medicaid can be a far more significant contributor.

Medicaid Long-Term Care Qualification and Provisions

When applying for Medicaid long-term care services, individuals generally need to have used up (i.e., spent down) or otherwise divested/gifted their assets more than five years ago. In most states, they need to have less than $2,000 in their name in order to qualify. At a glance, this requirement makes Medicaid seem like a service tailored exclusively for those in dire financial straits (a.k.a. "poor people").

However, the Medicaid code contains provisions designed to prevent the "community spouse" (the spouse not requiring care) from descending into poverty. In many states, assets up to $148,620 (amount for 2023; this number is generally adjusted annually for inflation) can be shielded from Medicaid scrutiny. Depending on the state, this protection can extend to either $148,620 or half of the total assets, whichever is less.

But there's another crucial aspect to consider: the *five-year lookback period*. Medicaid will meticulously examine bank statements, property deeds, DMV documents, and titles for boats and cars—essentially, everything in your name for the past five years (in every state except California, which only looks back thirty months). This rule means you can't merely transfer money to a spouse or children and expect to qualify for Medicaid the next day. If, during this period, you divested assets without receiving their market value in return, your Medicaid application would likely be denied. You'll have to properly and legally dispose of the asset in some way, or you won't qualify. Let's examine this process, referred to as the "Medicaid Spenddown."

How to Address Medicaid Spenddown

We just went over three key components that must be addressed during Medicaid planning: income limits, asset limits, and the five-year lookback period. In order to qualify, Medicaid will want you to spend down (or divest) your assets, meaning you'll need to figure out what to get rid of and what to keep. But how do you know what stays and what goes? The best place to start is by determining which of your assets are exempt and which are countable. We've presented examples of these categories in the image below.

Medicaid Spenddown:
Countable vs Non-Countable Assets

ALL assets from both spouses fit into 1 of 2 categories

Exempt Assets/ Non-Countable	Countable Assets
Principal Residence ($688,000 limit)	Other real estate
One Car	Checking & Savings
Personal Property	CDs & Money Market
Term Life Insurance	War and Savings Bongs
Cash value in whole life ins. policy $1,500 or less	Mutual Funds & Stocks
Pre-Paid Funeral	Fixed and Variable Annuities
Special Annuities	Retirement Assets (IRAs, 401(k), etc.)

In the image above, if your primary house is worth under $688,000 (amount for 2023; this number is generally adjusted annually for inflation), then it's exempt from the calculation. A handful of states, like New Jersey and Connecticut, use a higher equity limit of $1,033,000 (amount for 2023; also adjusted annually for inflation). Other items are exempt as well, including:

- One car
- Personal property (e.g., household belongings)
- Term life insurance policy
- Cash value in whole life insurance policy ($1,500 or less)
- Prepaid funeral
- Special annuities

So, what is countable? Well, everything else. This means all other real estate besides your principal residence (such as a second home), checking and savings accounts, savings bonds, money market accounts, mutual funds, stocks, fixed and variable annuities, and retirement assets. These types of assets must be dealt with properly or you will be forced to spend them down to the applicable Medicaid program limits.

Now, this may sound like a tough pill to swallow. If you have substantial assets, for example up to 500,000 dollars in assets, you may be thinking, "Do I really have to spend all this money before I qualify?" Fortunately, it's not exactly the way it works. To make it simple, you'll want to talk with a Medicaid planner, preferably a Certified Medicaid Planner™ or an elder law attorney. They should be able to legally restructure the countable resources in a way where they do not count toward the cap.

Medicaid Strategy in Action

Let's look at another scenario, this one involving a married couple by the names of Jim and Diane, who lived in North Carolina. Jim, at the age of eighty-four, began showing signs of cognitive decline. While his mind used to be like a steel trap, Diane noticed he had started becoming increasingly forgetful in the last few years. Additionally, Jim faced physical challenges. He underwent a knee replacement three years before and broke his leg in a fall two years later. As Jim was a good-sized guy, his wife found it challenging to take care of him fully at home. To give him the care he required, she realized she needed assistance. So they got an at-home care nurse to come in and help.

One unfortunate day, Jim fell. His nurse couldn't lift him up, resulting in a 911 call and hospital admission. To make matters worse, he had a bladder infection, which caused him to experience delirium. After his medical treatment, Jim was sent to a rehab facility to recover and regain mobility. The plan was a short-term stay for Jim, for which Medicare would have covered the costs. However, just three days into his rehabilitation, Jim's dementia worsened, making him combative and causing him to refuse rehab. As a result, Medicare stopped its coverage. This left Diane with a massive bill. If she wished for Jim to stay at the facility, she would have to bear the cost of $9,000 a month.

Diane and Jim had not purchased a long-term care policy. Without this coverage, Diane faced a significant financial burden. The couple's assets amounted to $380,000, not including their home. If she chose the straightforward route, she would be spending $108,000 annually on Jim's care, effectively depleting their assets within a few years. Of the $380,000, Medicaid provisions would allow Diane to retain $148,620. However, this meant a "spenddown" of the remaining $241,000 over approximately two years. Once the money was spent down, Jim would qualify for Medicaid.

Without hesitation, our Certified Medicaid Planner™ colleagues jumped in, ready to do what could be done to help the couple retain their assets. The strategy was to move the $148,620 to Diane's name for protection. The remaining $231,000 was used to purchase an actuarially sound Medicaid qualified annuity. This type of annuity is designed to be compliant with Medicaid's rules. By doing this, they effectively made the $231,000 non-countable against the Medicaid asset tests; moreover, the income generated from this annuity would be Diane's to keep.

By following this plan, Jim's cost of care (originally $9,000 per month) was offset by his $2,500 per month Social Security income, which would go toward the nursing home. This strategy saved them $6,500 monthly (being paid by Medicaid) that would otherwise have been taken from their assets. In addition to addressing her husband's care needs, Diane would have a continued source of income from the annuity. This gave them an immense sense of relief, establishing a secure way to fund Jim's care and the couple's other life expenses.

Medicaid Strategy for the Single Individual—Half a Loaf

But what about those who aren't married? For such a situation, let's look at a case involving a single client, Evelyn. Evelyn resided in a nursing home in West Virginia, where she incurred expenses of $10,500 per month. With an income of just $2,000 monthly, the difference (a substantial $8,500) was being drawn from her savings. With only $98,000 left in her account and a monthly depletion rate of $8,500, she faced a rapidly dwindling cash reserve. Evelyn's distress was palpable; she earnestly desired to leave her savings to her children, but on her current path, the situation wasn't looking good. Her money would be quickly used up for the cost of care.

Medicaid rules are stringent and you could even say complex, but there are certain provisions, if and when applied by a professional, that can work in the beneficiary's favor. One such strategy involves applying for Medicaid, intentionally getting denied due to excess assets, and simultaneously strategically reallocating those assets to make sure care costs are covered.

In Evelyn's case, the team intentionally "stirred the pot" *wi*th Medicaid. Similar to a hockey player causing a ruckus on the ice to gain an advantage during a close game, it was recommended Evelyn give half her money away to her children, *which would intentionally incur a Medicaid penalty*. The penalty in hockey is usually a few minutes off the ice. But this penalty for Evelyn would amount to longer time out of Medicaid: five months of ineligibility. Medicaid would not cover the bills for the next five months after the application was filed. While it may sound bad, this was all part of a precisely calculated plan. (This is called the *Half a Loaf* strategy because Evelyn was able to protect roughly half of her assets.)

The remaining half of Evelyn's savings, which wasn't given away, was transformed into a short-term Medicaid-compliant annuity. This annuity was structured to pay out directly to the nursing home over the duration of the five-month penalty. By the time the penalty period concluded, the annuity was exhausted. At the end of this penalty period, Evelyn was eligible for Medicaid.

But what about the half gifted to Evelyn's children? Well, it was thought out too. That money was untouched and completely safe. Her children could spend it as they saw fit, honoring Evelyn's wish to pass on a legacy. By navigating the rules of Medicaid carefully, Evelyn and her family were able to experience the best possible outcome available for her situation.

Navigating Medicaid Rules

If you're reading this book right now, it's possible you may be in a crisis just like Diane and Jim or Evelyn. Maybe you have a spouse who just received a dementia diagnosis or have a loved one who needs to be cared for in a nursing home or assisted living facility. No matter what the issue, reach out to us; we can direct you to the proper resources for assistance.

The rules of Medicaid are a complicated and confusing maze. I wouldn't say they are intentionally confusing, but sometimes it seems they are a bit inconsistent. Some states have their own set of unique rules, and to make matters even murkier, certain states have variations county by county. For the everyday individual to grasp and navigate this complex tapestry of rules and laws, I won't go as far as to say it's impossible, but it's akin to finding a needle in a haystack. It will almost certainly be a daunting task to complete.

This is why, when individuals collaborate with us, and we stumble upon such predicaments, we urge them to gather their allies. In addition to a financial and Medicaid planner, you may also want an attorney. The combined expertise of this team can be invaluable when formulating a plan to safeguard your assets, which is the crux of our entire endeavor here. Jumping through these bureaucratic hoops isn't fun, but it's necessary, especially if you want your assets to go where they rightfully belong rather than being absorbed by a nursing home. We've been through hundreds of these cases and in our years of experience, we've encountered nearly every scenario you can think of. In the end, our strategies can help you secure and safeguard your assets that, without our intervention, might have been left exposed.

Safeguarding Your Home from Medicaid Estate Recovery

Because of just how complex Medicaid planning can be, having an expert guide can be invaluable, especially when you come up against challenges such as Medicaid Estate Recovery (MER). This program seeks to recoup long-term care costs by taking assets such as a deceased person's home. This is akin to reaching into your pockets after you are in the grave. Consider this scenario: You own a house valued at half a million dollars, and the care you've received costs $200,000. Without appropriate measures taken in advance, the state could later enforce the sale of the house to retrieve the care expenses.

But wait, wasn't a house valued under $688,000 an exempt asset? This is true up until the point where the person receiving care dies. But here is where it gets tricky: Even if the home initially fits the exemption criteria, some states won't shy away from aggressively recovering against its value after the patient's death or the second spouse's death. Your loved ones may very well have to deal with Medicaid trying to take your home after you pass to recoup the costs of care.

The point is that there are solutions to Medicaid-related problems to serve as shields against potential clawbacks. While these techniques aren't always public knowledge, in most cases, the colleagues we partner with and work beside know exactly what to do. This expertise has consistently proven invaluable in many cases, ensuring at least 50 percent (and in many scenarios, up to 100 percent) of assets remain protected.

As you navigate the complexities of Medicaid planning, it's vital to remember two things:

1. You're not without options.
2. You're not without help. The team we have assembled is by your side, so you won't have to navigate these treacherous waters alone.

From Immediate Medical Needs to Estate Planning: Dealing with Wills, Trusts, and Living Documents

Since we've covered what you need to know about long-term care and Medicaid, it's time to take a closer look at a bit of a sensitive subject: how to prepare for incapacitation and death. Preparing living and after-life documents isn't just about money; it's about being able to make decisions to guide your loved ones when you aren't there to guide them yourself. In our next chapter, we'll look at what documents you'll need, why they are important, and what it means to select beneficiaries.

9

While You're Alive and After You're Gone

Wills, Trusts, and Living Documents

Living documents, wills, and trusts are all vital components of a comprehensive retirement plan. These instruments can act as our voice when we are unable to speak, helping us maintain control and decision-making capabilities regarding our finances, health, and more, even in unforeseen circumstances.

It cannot be overstated that someone with legal expertise must carefully draft and implement these documents. Yes, you may be able to find templates online for some, but those will be generic and may not cover the specific laws in your state. Attempting to complete these documents without proper training could lead to discrepancies, invalid provisions, or poorly structured directives. To avoid these complications, *I firmly believe in seeking legal counsel to ensure your will, trusts, and living documents are accurate, thorough, and legally sound.*

Let me illustrate the importance of these instruments with the story of a unique trust I dealt with. A client by the name of Sally had just retired from a fulfilling career as a nurse. She was dealing with the loss of her husband, who had passed away after a lengthy battle with cancer a couple of years before she came to see us. When Sally retired and came to me for financial advice, I pointed her to an attorney to get her affairs in order. One of the documents the attorney prepared during this time was a will including detailed provisions for the care of one of her closest friends . . . her horse.

You see, this particular breed of horse could live to be twenty-five to thirty years old, especially when well cared for. So, Sally's will included provisions to set up a trust, which included everything her horse might need: regular veterinary care, quality feed, and comfortable accommodations. She planned for a generous $1,000 a month to ensure her horse would be taken care of if she was no longer there to do so herself. Now, that's what I call foresight.

Sally's story serves as more than just a touching anecdote; it's a valuable lesson on the essential role of retirement planning elements, like trusts. We must plan for all possible contingencies, no matter how difficult they may be to contemplate. By taking these necessary steps, we can protect the people (or animals) we love most after we're gone.

Trusts are only one part of the broader estate planning puzzle, though. As we delve further into this subject, we'll explore the five fundamental documents I believe everyone should possess. These can be categorized into living documents, which take effect during our lifetime, and post-life documents, which govern what happens after our passing.

Living and Post-Life Documents
Living Document #1: Durable Power of Attorney

The *durable power of attorney*, which some people call the *financial power of attorney*, isn't just about finances. This document assigns a chosen individual the power to handle your financial and nonfinancial affairs should you become incapacitated. This means it can act as a safety net in the event you get in an accident or come down with a serious illness. I've had calls from clients saying, "Hey Joe, my mom had a stroke, and we need to get a power of attorney from her." This is when I have to say, "Well, hold on now. You can't just get a power of attorney; it has to be given to you by the individual." So, if a client or one of their children rings me up and says they need a power of attorney for their parents, it's often too late. This needs to be done while you're still of sound mind.

Let's think about the alternative: If you fail to give someone this authority, and you then become incapacitated and can't make decisions, someone would be forced to petition a judge to declare you incompetent. That's a rough process. You can look in the news to see examples of a billionaire's adult children trying to prove their parent has lost his or her marbles so they can declare them incompetent and get control of their money. These stories can make people worry about giving power of attorney, but don't worry—if the person becomes unreliable, you can rescind it and give it to someone else. It's a living document, not a dead one!

Just a side note here: This document isn't only important for those approaching retirement. Young adults and college-aged kids who aren't married yet should also consider setting up a durable power of attorney. If you have adult children who lack this safeguard, unforeseen incidents could lead to complex legal challenges.

Living Document #2: Healthcare Power of Attorney

The *healthcare power of attorney* is a document that has become increasingly crucial in the last decade with changes in privacy laws. One critical law relating to healthcare power of attorney is the Health Insurance Portability and Accountability Act (HIPAA). Because of federal HIPAA laws, doctors and hospitals cannot share certain information without an individual's consent. This restriction even applies to sharing details with family members. If a family member or other individual needs access to this information, they would require authorization through a healthcare power of attorney or other legally compliant means.

You would also need a healthcare power of attorney if you wanted a person to be able to act as your advocate and make healthcare-related decisions. Once a person has been selected as your advocate, they will be able to manage your healthcare needs, taking care of everything from the medication you get to the doctors who provide your care.

Living Document #3: Living Will

While the term "will" often brings to mind a single legal document distributing assets after a person's death, it isn't the only type you'll need. Yes, there is a will you'll have after you pass, but there is also a helpful document while you are still around: your *living will*. A living will is a statement written by you detailing what should be done if you become incapacitated, mentally incompetent, or are no longer able to communicate your wishes. If your health gets to the point where it seems there is no return, a living will states whether or not you want any extraordinary measures to be used to keep you alive.

One of the primary purposes of the living will is to serve as the "pull the plug document." What you are saying with this document is, essentially, "If I get to the point where all my organs are failing or I'm going to be a vegetable living on a machine, then please let me go." It can be paired with a DNR (Do Not Resuscitate), a medical document instructing medical staff to avoid CPR if your heart or breathing stops. Now again, I'm not an attorney; I'm just trying to provide you with all your options. You will need to talk with an attorney about the exact way these documents will work.

Post-Life Document #1: Simple Will (or Last Will and Testament)

The first of our post-life documents is a *simple will*. This document will allow you to name your beneficiaries or the loved ones who will inherit your belongings. These belongings can vary but may include property, vehicles, money, family heirlooms, and anything else you may want to leave to those close to you. If you have any children still considered minors, you will also designate their guardians (though the courts may have a say concerning the children's best interest). Choosing guardians is a big responsibility, so carefully considering who you select is important.

To ensure your wishes are carried out, you'll need to assign an executor. Your executor will handle all business relating to settling your estate, including distributing your possessions and paying off any remaining debts. The executor, along with your will, can help resolve any disputes the living may have about who gets your possessions. You can also entrust your executor to organize your funeral arrangements by leaving special instructions elsewhere in your will. You may consider adding in your will that the executor does not need to be bonded, thus saving them the hassle and financial burden of paying for this specific service.

Another element to consider with a will is the process of *probate*. This means everything within your will must be proven and certified. Completing the process can mean a notice will be published to make the will a matter of public record, which may open doors for claims against your estate to contest your will. If you have an old debt, someone can come in and make a claim against your estate. In addition, if your children don't like the way things are being distributed, they can also contest the will.

Of course, minimizing or avoiding the probate process can be possible, particularly when privacy or the quicker distribution of assets is a concern. One of the best ways to do this is through the establishment of certain types of trusts.

Post-Life Document #2: Trust

The final piece of the puzzle is a *trust*. The trust most people set up is what's known as a *revocable living trust*. This type of trust is created while you're alive, and "revocable" means you have the flexibility to make adjustments to it while you are alive. You retain complete control over your assets, whether it's buying or selling real estate or cars or moving money around, and you still have full control to determine what to do with all of your money and possessions.

The real power of a revocable living trust comes into play upon your death when it turns into an *irrevocable trust*. At that point, the terms of the trust are set in stone, and it becomes virtually impossible for anyone to challenge the way the assets are distributed. This is because the trust doesn't have to go through the public and often a lengthy legal process of probate.

There are three primary advantages of the revocable living trust:

1. It avoids probate, which saves time and potentially money.
2. It's less likely to be contested, providing a firm plan for your assets.
3. It provides that a designated trustee will ensure the contents of the trust are distributed according to your instructions.

Contrast this with a will, which passes through the public probate process, while with a trust, the trustee does not have to do anything at the courthouse. However, they are bound by the document itself to make sure the terms are executed as specified.

In essence, a revocable living trust provides a secure, private, and efficient way to manage and distribute your estate. It's worth noting that while each person in a married couple should have individual documents, such as powers of attorney and healthcare directives, they can often start with just one trust for both parties. This type of trust can be a foundational piece to, and key part of, a sound estate plan.

Other Types of Trusts

While a revocable living trust is important, it isn't the only type of trust you may need. Here is an overview of a few other variations that may come in handy.

- **Children's Trust:** This trust is designed for families with minor children. Should both parents pass away, a trust can be set up to manage the children's financial needs until they come of age. Provisions can be included to dictate how much money is distributed and when, ensuring the funds are used for their health, education, and maintenance. It's common to stagger distributions, releasing funds at ages twenty-one, twenty-five, or thirty to ensure financial stability and wise decision-making on behalf of the children. This type of trust is typically included within the parent's will.
- **Special Needs Trust:** If there are children or adults with special needs in the family, this trust ensures they are cared for. Recognizing that they

may not be able to care for themselves, a special needs trust can hold and manage assets on their behalf, providing support for their entire lifetime without an end date. In addition, a special needs trust may ensure that the special needs child is able to stay on government programs designed for their care. If too many assets flow to a special needs child, these vital benefits could be interrupted or lost.
- **Pet Trust:** As the story of Sally and her horse shows us, pet trusts are not only real, but part of a growing trend. These unique trusts are established to ensure beloved pets are cared for after their owner's death. The trust can designate a caregiver for the pet and outline the specific care requirements. A very important role of the trust is to allocate a specific range of money for the pet's care. This trust isn't limited to common pets such as dogs or cats; it can even extend to animals with much longer life spans, for instance, horses (which can live twenty-five to thirty years) or certain types of birds, which can live even longer.

These trusts can provide tailored solutions for unique family situations. Whether safeguarding your children's financial future, ensuring the care of special needs family members, or providing for beloved pets, trusts can also add additional protection and peace of mind in estate planning. By considering the particular needs and circumstances of your loved ones, you can create trusts to align with your values and intentions.

In addition, there are numerous types of irrevocable trusts which people use to transfer assets outside of their estate for various reasons (notably, qualifying for Medicaid and potentially minimizing estate taxes); however, they are beyond the scope of this book.

Beneficiary Designations

When we talk about the beneficiaries of assets, their role in estate planning can't be overstated. This is especially true when it comes to dealing with bank accounts, brokerage accounts, insurance policies, pensions, 401(k)s, or other retirement accounts. These designations determine who will receive the assets in these accounts after your death. ***Warning: Beneficiary designations take precedence over other methods of asset distribution, and they are virtually impossible to alter after the fact.***

To illustrate the significance of keeping beneficiary designations up to date, let's consider the story of Martha, a schoolteacher. Martha got married in her thirties to Samuel, and they enjoyed a wonderful marriage. Tragically, Martha was diagnosed with cancer and passed away at age fifty-five. During her teaching career, she listed her sister as the sole beneficiary of her life insurance and retirement account. After her marriage to Samuel, she failed to update the beneficiary information.

When Martha passed away, her husband, expecting to receive nearly a million dollars from the retirement plan, discovered that the beneficiary was still Martha's sister. Despite his pleas, Martha's sister refused to relinquish the funds, claiming they were rightfully hers. Sadly, after a lengthy and heated legal action, the beneficiary designation was upheld, and Martha's sister received all the money while Martha's husband, Samuel, received nothing.

This story serves as a stark reminder to review and update beneficiary designations regularly, especially when major life changes such as marriage, divorce, or death occur. Once a person passes away, these designations cannot be changed. So, keeping them current is *crucial* to ensure that assets are distributed according to one's wishes.

Our firm prioritizes discussions with clients about their beneficiary designations when they first come on board. We encourage and guide them in examining every designation to avoid problems similar to the one faced by Martha and Samuel. It's a critical step in effective estate planning and one that absolutely and periodically needs to be addressed.

Leaving a Mark: From Trusts and Wills to Legacy and Life Insurance Planning

Trusts and wills are vital tools that can ensure your assets are distributed according to your wishes. They lay the groundwork for a thoughtful and well-structured estate plan, but they are only part of the broader picture. You'll also want to think about the legacy you want to leave behind and what financial instruments can make your legacy a reality.

In our next chapter, we will dive into the world of legacy and life insurance planning. We'll explore the tools to complement your will and trust planning, providing additional layers of protection and opportunities for growth. Whether you're seeking to leave an inheritance, support charitable causes, or ensure your loved ones have the resources they need, life insurance and legacy planning provide the flexibility and foresight to make those dreams a reality.

10

Legacy and Life Insurance Planning

Here is something many find surprising to learn: Only 52 percent of Americans have life insurance.[14] This statistic reflects just how many people overlook one of the most vital tools in estate and legacy planning. While some may perceive life insurance simply as a safety net, it's so much more. Life insurance is a multifaceted instrument to ensure your loved one's well-being, provide for long-term care (as we discussed in chapter 7) and even facilitate your ability to champion charitable causes. But it can do even more, extending well beyond these conventional uses.

---

14 Crail, C. (2023, June 21). "Life Insurance Statistics, Data, and Industry Trends" 2023. *Forbes Advisor*. https://www.forbes.com/advisor/life-insurance/life-insurance-statistics/

My perspective on the matter is that properly structured life insurance, specifically that which is built into a retirement estate plan, gives you something invaluable: *the permission to spend your money.* Let's take a moment to let this sink in because it really is important. When you have the right amount of life insurance in place, you are no longer bound by the anxiety of spending down your savings. Don't get me wrong, I'm not saying you should start recklessly swiping your credit card with abandon—I'm talking about enjoying the fruits of your labor.

Imagine this: You've worked hard all your life, saved, and invested wisely. Now you've reached a point where you want to enjoy some of those savings, but you are concerned about leaving something behind for your heirs. What if you could spend down to the last $10,000, $20,000, or even $50,000 and still know a significant life insurance sum will be sitting there when you pass away? This is the type of assurance that life insurance can potentially provide.

We're talking about a mindset change here, specifically, the freedom to secure your financial legacy while letting you live fully in the present. It's like having a strong safety harness that allows you to walk the tightrope of life with total confidence. You can explore, experience, and embrace your golden years without the nagging worry that you're eating into your children's or grandchildren's inheritance. It's all about striking the right balance, ensuring that your money serves you in life and continues to serve your values and loved ones after you're gone.

Choosing a Type of Life Insurance

When we're examining life insurance, a critical question arises: Which type should you get? Essentially, there are two categories here: **term** and **permanent**. Each type has its merits, but choosing the right one for your specific needs requires a keen understanding of their fundamental differences.

Let's start with **term insurance**. This type of policy covers you for a designated period, usually five, ten, or twenty years. When that period is over, the term expires, and you're no longer covered. Think of it like renting coverage for a set number of years. The downside is unless you have the magical ability to predict the exact moment of your passing and can time it perfectly (a feat almost impossible to achieve), term insurance makes it hard to leave a specific sum behind.

That said, term insurance definitely has its advantages. People often choose term because it is less expensive. You may be asking, "Why is it more affordable?" Well, for two main reasons. First, it only covers you for a specific amount of time. Second, the percentage of term policies paying out versus the number of permanent policies paying out is significant. In fact, you might be surprised to learn that 99 percent of all term policies never pay a death benefit.[15] Insurance companies know this, and certainly use it to their advantage, but it doesn't mean you shouldn't have term insurance. If you feel the need to shield your family

---

15 Pope, C. (2023). "*Term Life Insurance*". *Bankrate*. https://www.bankrate.com/insurance/life-insurance/term-life-insurance/

or safeguard future earning capabilities with extensive coverage, term insurance can be quite useful.

However, if your heart is set on guaranteeing a particular amount of money when you pass, then it would be best to consider **permanent insurance**. Unlike term, permanent insurance doesn't run out; it's similar to owning a lifetime of coverage. You can think of term insurance as renting a house and permanent insurance as buying. Of course, just as with buying a house, permanent insurance can come with a higher price tag. But if it matches more closely with your goals and values, then it can be well worth the price.

Life Insurance Beneficiaries

Far from being just a footnote in a financial plan, beneficiaries can be one of the most vital parts of establishing the legacy you want. We touched on this subject in the previous chapter, but it's worth reiterating the point. Whether it's an insurance policy, annuity, or retirement account, I would argue that the beneficiary designation is *the strongest* financial instrument you can employ to transfer an asset. This isn't a matter to take lightly. If you want a particular person to receive money, you must ensure they're the named beneficiary.

Now, here's where things can get a bit complex. Even if you've detailed your beneficiaries in a will or trust, the nature of the financial instrument (be it a life insurance policy, investment account, or annuity contract) means the first thing a company will look at is the beneficiary designation. Your will or trust might be a masterpiece of planning, but at the end of the day, the beneficiary designation is king.

In many cases, the investment or insurance company cares far less about the will; their eyes go straight to the beneficiary designation. If beneficiaries are designated, whomever you've listed is the one who'll get the money. Of course, if there is any discrepancy between the beneficiary designations in your insurance policy and what you have in your will or trust, then you've got a problem. The problem is that now what you wanted to happen after you are gone may not happen.

So, take the time to review and align your beneficiary designations and ensure they are consistent and reflect your true intentions. By doing so, you can avoid unnecessary confusion and make sure your assets go exactly where you want them to go.

The Unintended Consequences of Benefciary Designations

Allow me to share an example that shows the importance of proper beneficiary planning. I encountered a woman named Claire during my work in the cemetery business. Claire was in her second marriage, as was her husband, a man about twenty years her senior and already retired. They shared a home, but it was their only piece of joint property. Claire's husband had designated that his pension benefits and life insurance go to his first wife after his death. Claire was aware and accepting of this, not really considering the possible consequences. Here is where her story takes a tragic turn.

Although she knew about these designations, she had grown reliant on her husband's income. Their lifestyle was almost entirely supported by a combination of his money and Social Security benefits, a lifestyle that allowed them to live comfortably in the shared home. Then, her husband passed away. Her life was upended in an instant, and she had to make tough decisions she never anticipated. As expected, his pension and life insurance went to his previous wife, leaving Claire surviving only on her own limited income. Faced with the cold reality of financial strain, she had no choice but to sell the home they had shared for so many years. If the proper beneficiary designations had been in place or she had placed the proper amount of life insurance on her husband, the situation could have turned out much more favorably for her, and she may have been able to keep her home.

This story isn't meant to sadden you but rather to underscore a crucial point: Financial planning, especially regarding beneficiaries and life insurance, isn't just about legalities. It's about understanding the real-world consequences of those choices. *Today's decisions can profoundly affect your loved ones' tomorrows.*

Crafting Your Legacy

When we talk about legacy, we're delving into what you leave behind. Legacy isn't just about numbers—it's about people, emotions, and the fabric of families. We've talked before about the average time it takes for an inheritance to be spent, but another topic some people forget is how an inheritance should be split. The question is: Should your inheritance be split equally among your heirs?

Let's take a hypothetical scenario. Suppose you have four children. Most people would say that each kid should get 25 percent. On the surface, that seems fair, but life isn't always that simple. You also have to look at the situations each child is facing in their lives. What if one of your children has a highly successful business, while another has battled with substance abuse all her life? Should their inheritance still be equal? Do you give the child struggling with addiction immediate access to all their money? Or do you put it in a trust, allowing a responsible family member to control it, ensuring that the funds don't lead to self-destruction? This may seem like a logical path, but even the best decisions could lead to animosity. These are all things to consider when creating your estate plan.

There are a number of different scenarios where you may have to take specific considerations into account. For example, one of your children may have special needs. While an equal share may still be appropriate, direct access to the money might not be. Leaving the funds to someone who can ensure your child with special needs gets the support they need will be important.

Given the emotional and financial complexities of these decisions, it's often helpful to seek the guidance of a financial planner or estate planning professional. They can offer an objective perspective, help navigate those murky family conflicts, and ensure the estate plan aligns with your wishes and the heirs' best interests.

Let's look at an example. I had a client, Stephanie, who faced a complex and delicate situation. She had two daughters, two years apart in age. One of them had always been financially conservative, a great saver who had paid off her house and had a stable retirement. The other daughter, well, let's just say she had never met a dollar she couldn't spend.

So, Stephanie had a tough decision to make. She decided on an even split—half the estate to her financially fit daughter and the other half to her second daughter, who wasn't as financially savvy. But instead of handing over the money directly, Stephanie left it in a trust administered by her financially fit daughter. As you can imagine, this decision created years of tension between the sisters. It's the kind of decision that can sour relationships, even though it was made to protect someone she loved. Stephanie knew her less financially responsible daughter would spend the money immediately and might end up worse off than when she started.

The trust created animosity and strained the sisters' relationship, but it did fulfill its purpose. When the daughter who had struggled financially passed away twenty-five years later, the house she inherited went to her kids. She may have resented her mother and sister for the decision, but it ensured that her children would inherit something valuable. Sometimes setting up a trust isn't about doubting someone's abilities or integrity. It's about protecting them, even when they don't realize they need protection.

What If I Have No Children?

So, let's look at a situation often overlooked but equally important: What happens if you don't have any children? Well, that certainly doesn't mean you won't leave a legacy. Some clients choose to leave their belongings to nieces and nephews or other family members. Other clients choose to leave their money to the organizations that have meant the most to them in life. Some make organizations that reflect their passions and beliefs their beneficiaries. I remember one client whose heroes were the NRA and his church, and he chose to leave each about a million dollars equally.

Now, some of these folks prefer to keep their charitable giving entirely anonymous, and I can respect that. But I'd like to offer another perspective. You've worked hard all your life, and if you're planning to leave a substantial part of your estate to a cause you believe in, such as your local church or favorite charity, why not let them know?

I'm a firm believer that there's something to be said for receiving recognition for your generosity while you're still breathing. It's not about ego; it's about celebrating the impact your hard-earned money can make in the world. You want to be remembered for something positive that speaks to your values and beliefs, and if an act can be celebrated and acknowledged while you're still around to see it, well, I think that's a beautiful thing.

For those without direct heirs, or even those with them, another meaningful way to leave a legacy is by considering how you might impact the broader community or support future generations. One way to do this is through the establishment of a scholarship.

Scholarships

Scholarships are an excellent way to help support students who may be struggling financially. You can base your scholarship on almost anything: a sport you were fond of in school, a field of study you enjoy, or a talent you think is important to encourage. You would define what you want your scholarship to be, set the amount of funding it provides and for what length of time, and choose an institution to partner with. If you decide to do this while you are still around, you may even be able to help choose the recipients!

When considering the creation of a scholarship, it's vital to ensure this aligns with your overall legacy vision. If you have children or other dependents, their expectations might influence your decision. A scholarship can be a wonderful thing, but it's not a decision to be made lightly or quickly. In most cases, this isn't a ten-minute conversation, but rather a series of deep discussions. It's best to talk it out with your spouse, attorney, or financial advisor. We can help you explore any questions you have about the process, consider options you may not think about, and guide you through the specific steps involved.

No Matter What Your Choice Is, Planning Is Key

I can't emphasize enough how important it is to be up-front and proactive in the planning process. When we get all these details squared away, it means you don't have to worry about it later.

Of course, life is rarely static, and situations can change. For example, I have had clients whose beneficiary was "excommunicated" from the family. These scenarios are why revisiting legacy plans is important. We look over my clients' plans periodically (generally every few years) to ensure everything is current and in line with their wishes.

In the end, leaving a legacy isn't just about what happens after we're gone; it's about how we live our lives, how we connect with the causes we care about, and how we're remembered by those who come after us. It's an intimate and personal decision and one I encourage everyone to think about deeply and discuss openly with those involved. After all, a legacy is a reflection of a life well lived, and it deserves to be crafted with care and intention.

Reflecting on Our Journey

Financial planning isn't just about numbers on a spreadsheet or dollars in a bank account. It's deeply intertwined with our aspirations, dreams, families, and lasting imprints we wish to leave behind. Now, as we prepare to close this book, let's take a step back and reflect on the big picture, highlight some key takeaways from each chapter, and discuss how you can move forward from here.

Conclusion

As we look back on the numerous topics we covered, you may wonder, "How am I supposed to remember all this stuff when I'm planning my own retirement?" To be completely honest, you may not be able to. I've worked for decades to gain an understanding of financial planning, and without the guidance of a professional, it's easy to get lost in the weeds. But to help you review some of the main points, let's look back at the key concepts we covered in each chapter.

Chapter 1: It's Not a Budget, It's a Spending Plan: How to Determine Your Core Expenses

In this chapter, we tackled the topic of spending plans and how to identify your major expenses. These expenses often include:

- housing
- utilities
- medical costs
- insurance
- food
- transportation

We also discussed the hidden costs many folks overlook and separating the things we want from the things we need. Crafting a good spending plan means taking a long, hard look at the essentials and addressing easier-to-cut areas such as vice spending.

Chapter 2: Income Planning Part 1: Maximizing Your Social Security Benefits

In our first income planning section, we took a look at one of the primary ways to generate income in retirement: Social Security benefits. I showed you a few statistics illustrating just how important Social Security is before diving into the potential cuts the program is facing in the future. We also discussed a few fixes to save the Social Security program, including:

- Payroll tax rate increases
- Retirement age adjustments
- Income cap raises
- COLA formula changes

We then did a deep dive into the definition of full retirement age, how waiting to take your benefit can be beneficial, and how you can work and collect Social Security at the same time. The chapter closed with an explanation of the taxes surrounding Social Security and spousal benefits, as well as the best ways to keep up to date on Social Security news.

Chapter 3: Income Planning Part 2: Pensions 101 and the Rise of the 401(k) Plan

The second part of our income planning section addressed pensions and 401(k) plans. I began this chapter by talking about the creation of both of these instruments and highlighting the importance of the Revenue Act of 1978 and the father of the 401(k) plan, Ted Benna. As the 401(k) plan has risen, pensions have begun to vanish. Fortunately, there are modern alternatives, e.g., the cash balance plan, which can offer benefits and flexibility.

We also covered how to take your pension and the different joint life variations you can explore. We then dove into income maximization through the creation of a private annuity based income plan before addressing the different types of annuities you can utilize: **variable**, **fixed**, and **fixed index**.

Chapter 4: Asset Protection and Investment Planning: Cash, Income and Growth

Our last income planning section delved into the three primary planning buckets we use to protect assets and plan investments: **cash, income**, and **growth**.

- **Cash:** Liquid cash for expected and unexpected emergencies
- **Income:** Retirement income that is dependable and has the potential to increase over time

- **Growth (a.k.a. investment and recovery):** Investments designed to grow, replenish, and recover your principal without excessive risk

We broke down each and looked at a case study concerning Tim and Betty Johnson, which illustrated how we use these buckets to design our strategy. Chapter 4 closed with a section about the Risk Assessment system, which we use to ensure clients' current holdings match their risk tolerance.

Chapter 5: How to Structure Your Assets to Minimize Income Taxes

In chapter 5, we looked at the three categories of money: **taxable (nonqualified)**, **tax-deferred (qualified)**, or **tax-free**.

- **Taxable Accounts:** These include stocks, bonds, cash, savings accounts, certificates of deposit (CDs), and money market accounts. You must report and pay taxes on the majority of the growth these generate each year.
- **Tax-Deferred Accounts:** These include traditional IRAs, 401(k)s, and 403(b)s, government employees, thrift savings plans, as well as SIMPLE IRAs and SEP-IRAs. Tax-deferred accounts allow you to postpone paying taxes until later, which can help your money grow and compound.

- **Tax-Free Accounts:** These include Roth IRAs, Roth 401(k)s, and certain types of permanent life insurance. All growth and distributions from these accounts are tax-free when they are accessed properly.

While your account percentages may differ, a mix of 20 percent taxable, 40 percent tax-deferred, and 40 percent income tax-free offers several potential income tax benefits when distributions occur. The chapter went on to discuss the current tax code and tax planning strategies, including examples using our clients Mark and Brenda (who applied early for Social Security) and John and Connie (who applied more strategically). Chapter 5 closed by discussing positioning, withdrawal, and the best ways to move funds in a strategic manner.

Chapter 6: How to Plan and Save for Post-Retirement Fun

In chapter 6, we shifted gears and talked about the importance of having fun and staying active during retirement. Preparing for fun means getting everything in order at home, including deciding who will keep an eye on your house, mail, pets, and everything else you may worry about during your vacation. We also talked about the difference between leisure and travel as a retirement lifestyle, as well as the components and hidden costs you need to consider when doing either. The chapter concluded by talking about the need to overcome the guilt associated with spending. After all, you earned that money; you deserve to use it to have some fun!

Chapter 7: Reviewing Long-Term Healthcare Choices

In chapter 7, we discussed long-term care, starting with the six activities of daily living (ADLs) defining who qualifies for long-term care:

- Transferring
- Continence
- Bathing
- Dressing
- Toileting
- Eating

Afterward, we discussed the misconceptions surrounding long-term care and the two primary payment sources: private (personal assets and insurance) and public (Medicare, Veterans Aid and Attendance, and long-term Medicaid). From there, we dove into private pay, as well as deciding where and what type of care you may receive. Our chapter ended by talking about the Pension Protection Act and leveraging versus liquidation, specifically the primary ways to leverage your assets for care: traditional, life insurance-based, and hybrid long-term care plans.

Chapter 8: Medicaid Planning: It's Not Just for Poor People

Following up our long-term care chapter was chapter 8, which covered Medicaid planning. We discussed who qualifies and the provisions relating to Medicaid before touching on Medicaid spenddown, which involves divesting assets. I then showed you some Medicaid strategies we use to help our married and unmarried clients before covering how to navigate the rules surrounding Medicaid, including those relating to Medicaid estate recovery.

Chapter 9: Planning for Before and After: Living Documents, Wills, and Trusts

Chapter 9 delved into estate planning documentation, primarily living and post-life documents.

- **Living Documents:** Durable power of attorney, healthcare power of attorney, and living will
- **Post-Life Documents:** Simple will (or Last Will and Testament) and trusts

We covered revocable living trusts, which can help you avoid probate (saving you time and money), are virtually incontestable, and involve a designated trustee. I also told you about a few other types of trusts, including a children's trust, special needs trust, and pet trust. Our chapter closed with a discussion of beneficiary designations and just how important it is to choose the right beneficiary during estate planning.

Chapter 10: Legacy and Life Insurance Planning

Our final chapter was all about legacy and life insurance planning, starting with discussing the differences between term life insurance (a type of policy covering a designated period of time) and permanent life insurance (coverage lasting a lifetime). We touched on the subject of beneficiaries again, as well as the consequences of failing to make the correct designations. From there, we dove into legacies and how to decide the best ways to split up inheritances among children.

If you don't have children, don't worry, we also discussed other ways to establish a legacy, including leaving money to organizations and charities you are passionate about. Chapter 10 also covered setting up scholarships and ended by discussing the importance of legacy planning for leaving a lasting mark on this world after you are gone.

Staying Retired Can Be Simple with the Right Help

When it comes to financial planning, the most valuable thing isn't stocks, bonds, great life insurance, or strategic tax code utilization: **It's good advice.** Yes, all of those instruments can serve as the assets you'll need to StayRetired™, but without someone helping you steer the ship, money can leave as soon as it arrives. Life has a way of throwing curveballs when we least expect them. Markets fluctuate, personal situations evolve, and the rules of the game (e.g., tax laws and benefit structures) can change overnight. Venturing into this terrain alone can be daunting and, at times, overwhelming. This is where a financial planner steps in, not just as an advisor but as a partner in your journey.

We've helped countless clients from all income brackets figure out how to enjoy their retirement to the fullest, and we can help you too. With our experience and time-tested strategies, I have no doubt we can tackle any problem you experience. If you want to contact me for a free thirty-minute consultation or just to have a chat, you can find all my contact information below.

Contact Information

JOE ROSEMAN, JR.

Office Location: 5960 Fairview Road, Suite 400
Charlotte, North Carolina 28210
Email: jroseman@stayretiredwealth.com
Phone Number: (704) 935-2553
Website: http://www.stayretiredwealth.com/
Calendar Link: www.TalkToRoseman.com

Navigating life after retirement is no small task; doing it right requires patience, strategy, and, above all, proper guidance. As you close this book and reflect on your next steps, consider the value of having a seasoned partner by your side—someone who will celebrate your successes, help you overcome every challenge, and prioritize your best interests.

Let's embark on this journey together and craft a retirement where you feel not just secure in your future, but truly fulfilled in the present. With our help, you can sit back and relax as you enter your golden years. So, reach out today, and I'll show you just how easy it is to retire and, say it with me, **StayRetired™**.

About the Author

For over 30 years, **Joseph E Roseman Jr., "Joe"** to his clients, has developed easy-to-understand educational materials to assist hardworking Americans grow and preserve their wealth. Joe's goal for his clients is that they retire and StayRetired™. Joe hosts in-person seminars and online webinars on multiple retirement topics that include Social Security Maximization, Long-Term Care Planning, Tax Planning and Estate Planning. Joe feels that his clients deserve an education base so they can better understand and recognize a retirement, income and investment plan that is specific to their needs.

Every client has different circumstances, experiences, and assets. Joe is a *fiduciary* Financial Advisor acting only in the best interests of his clients and customizes every retirement and investment plan he provides. Having a customized plan allows his clients to have a roadmap for the specific type of retirement best suited for them and their lifestyle.

Joe has completed the course of study to earn the CRPC (Chartered Retirement Planning Consultant) designation. He has extensive knowledge of Federal Retirement Benefits and holds the ChFEBC (Chartered Federal Employee Benefits Consultant) designation. In addition, Joe has earned and holds the NSSA (National Social Security Advisor) designation for his work in helping clients maximize their Social Security benefits. Most recently, Joe completed requirements to hold the Certified Dementia Practitioner (CDP) designation by the National Council of Certified Dementia Practitioners.

Joe has been a guest on WBTV Channel 3, Charlotte, North Carolina, on their weekend morning news show and the evening news show, "On Your Side Tonight" with Jamie Boll, more than fifty times. He has contributed articles for and been quoted in *Time Magazine*, *US News and World Report*, and numerous other publications.

Joe was born and raised in Statesville, North Carolina. He graduated from UNC Chapel Hill with a Bachelor of Science Degree in Business Administration. Joe and his wife Debbie live in Charlotte, North Carolina, and have been happily married for over thirty-five years. They have a twenty-eight-year-old son and daughter-in-law who married in 2021. Their daughter, her husband, and their two daughters live in Northern California. Joe contributes and supports the Charlotte Rescue Mission. He and Debbie attend First Baptist Church Indian Trail.

Made in the USA
Columbia, SC
24 February 2024